BETWEEN FRIENDS

Between Friends

by Gillian E. Hanscombe

Sheba Feminist Publishers

First published in England 1983 by Sheba Feminist Publishers,
488 Kingsland Road, London E8 (01 254 1590)
First published 1982 in USA by Alyson Publications, Inc.,
Boston, Massachusetts.

Cover illustration and design by Sarah Pooley

Printed and bound by A Wheaton & Co Ltd, Exeter ·

for Elisabeth
with love

Meg to Frances

1 November

Dear Frances,

I can't quite understand why you haven't written for so long. Well, I can and I can't, let's put it that way. At our last meeting (a hundred years ago?) I felt the atmosphere to be uneasy — felt that you felt it too — but neither of us could quite come around to discussing it. Your fear of confrontation, perhaps, and my fear of your fear. I just remember your instant of frustration when you suddenly said 'Oh Meg, all this feminism. . . .' and that I felt hurt. Because you can't identify? It may be, though I don't want to admit it because it would make me seem dependent, as if I needed something from you that you don't need from me.

We seem to have been through this so many times, in so many places, in so many contexts. Do you remember watching that modern dance programme in New York and how I said to you afterwards that it was very stimulating but that only the men had real parts and the women were just props? And how you said you would never have thought of looking at it that way? And then one of our brief silences when we both don't know how to go on? Or looking at the Phyllis Chesler book — do you remember the picture of the statue where she remarks that the man is standing on a platform supported by several kneeling women — and you said, dismissively, 'Oh these feminists!' And so on. Somehow we always end up embattled — you on the defensive (is it *I* who attacks you?) and I feeling hurt (do you *mean* to hurt me?) — in an imitation of those ancient roles of proselytiser and unwilling listener. I don't want these roles. When I say what I see, I am saying only what I see, not preaching an ideology that has some existence outside me. And you are my friend, yet you seem not to believe that I tell you my own thoughts and feelings — that they are really mine.

When we don't talk about 'feminism' (or when you think we are not talking about it) we are both able to relax into each other's warmth and interest, able to feel our individuality, able to acknowledge the deep bond that has joined us over all these years. If neither of us had ever heard of 'feminism', and especially if you hadn't, I fantasise that you would have accepted that I see what I see and not rejected my vision. And that you would have done so because you were my friend. And that you would have felt, as friends do, that what I see contains at least some part of the truth, because of its consistency and because of the strength of my conviction. But as it is, 'feminism' exists and has my loyalty. And somehow inexplicably divides us.

You've always said you weren't worried by my being a lesbian — that our friendship was special and beyond sex — that your heterosexuality would not obstruct our friendship. But during these months of silence from you I've thought — although previously I agreed with your view — that there must somehow be a connection. You say my lesbianism doesn't bother you because it is part of my individuality and that you accept me as I am; on the other hand, my feminism is somehow not part of me, in your view, so you need to dissociate yourself from it. But it seems to me that lesbianism is a centre piece of the women's movement — so I thought, to be sympathetic to feminism, for you, probably means identifying yourself in some way with lesbianism (its stereotyped man-hating posture) which is what you have never done in your relationship with me.

You've always said my being a lesbian is private to me and your being heterosexual is private to you and that our friendship lies elsewhere — outside sexuality. But Frances, it seems to me that it can't and it doesn't — our being women is central to our mutuality, as well as being central to our individuality. We're not disembodied 'people' or 'personalities'; our thoughts, feelings, perceptions — everything is coloured with our female colours. The irony is that that is the very thing that most draws us to each other — the fact that we can understand each other's way of perceiving. So how *can* our sexuality not be an integral part of our relationship? I don't mean that we have to go to bed with each other — I mean we have to be more honest about what binds us so intimately together.

I think this conflict between us (yes, it *is* a conflict) is part of the reason why feminism hasn't caught on. Hundreds of women are constantly saying they support the social reforms the women's movement has asked for — equal pay, abortion rights, contraception, and so on — you have yourself — but they add hastily 'But I'm not a women's libber' or 'I don't agree with feminism'. That is what you've said to me so often. If women support social reforms but reject 'feminism', what exactly is it they are rejecting? It must be lesbianism, I thought — the fear of being forced to go to bed with women and the conviction of not wanting to 'reject men'. I am lately so full of new ideas about this, so urgently in need of your confidence and your commitment to our friendship, so wanting you to share with me the things you have always held back. . . please write. I can't possibly get to Canada before next summer and that's nine months away. Please believe me — it just can't wait till then.

I miss you so much, as well. Will you write?

Meg

ह•

Frances to Meg

28 December

Dear Meg,

I'm sorry it's taken me so long to answer your letter. I've been busy — the usual things — but I was also cowering

under the weight of your expectations and your old intensity,
which I thought we'd managed to come through, finally.

I was shocked by your letter. I'm sorry to be brutal about it
but you've asked for honesty and I want to be honest with
you. You seem to be inventing a conflict that doesn't exist for
me — I've always said your lesbian affairs are nothing to do
with me and even that I can't really understand what you feel
in that area. I refuse to let you tell me that my attitudes
towards feminism are conditioned by my (unconscious) fear of
your lesbianism. I haven't rejected you — but I reserve the
right to reject what you think sometimes, especially when it
seems to me to be obsessively concerned with only one
element of reality. I do *not* live and breathe through my
sexuality — and it *is*, in particular, your *mind* I've always
admired and respected. It doesn't make any difference to me
that you are female — you could have been a man and I would
still have responded to the parts of your personality I like so
much. And I *do* think you hate men, deeply, and that you
hate them because your father treated you so badly — and
that feminists are more or less like you — i.e. they've all been
treated badly by some man or other and therefore hate the
whole male half of the species. But life hasn't been like that
for me and I can't, even if I wanted to, see everything human
divided up into a war between men and women in which men
always win. I'm sorry you had a bad time with your father but
you mustn't expect me to think all men are savages just
because of that.

I want our friendship to be *personal* — not overlaid and
twisted about and distorted and intellectually manipulated by
a creed that is not my own. When you do that, you do something *to me*: you take something that is *mine* — my friendship for you — and you take it without asking me if you
may — and then you turn it into some experiment or some
example or I don't know what — which can be used to
demonstrate your theories about human society. I know you
well enough to know that you will also end up demonstrating
how awful men are and that that will cause a tremendous

difficulty between us. Please Meg, leave it alone. Let me be. I like my view of the world and anyway I have a right to it. Please leave me out of your feminism, just as you would leave me out of your Catholicism, or your Marxism, or any other ism you might otherwise have. If I were afraid of lesbianism, I wouldn't be able to be your friend. Can't you see that? Is that too simple for your hungry intellect?

We can, anyway, meet sooner than you thought. Jim has just won a grant to study in Paris for a year, starting on April 1. I can get to London for a fortnight or so then, if it suits you to put me up. I'm so longing for a week full of our usual chat/theatre/eating out — and to catch up on how your work is going... and Simon... God, you write to me about things in your head and tell me nothing about your life, which makes me feel out of contact with you and cheated of your warmth. I'm your *friend*, Meg — I'm not a woman's consciousness-raising group or whatever they do. Please write soon and tell me whether I can stay with you, and how Simon is, and the house, and your book — there's so much I want to know. I want to be able to imagine you living your life — can you *not* understand that?

As for me: New York was very satisfying. I made a lot of contacts, got a great haul of material from an old biddy who knew J.S. and I've just got a grant from one of the university foundations to pay for someone to catalogue the stuff. Paris will really be a waste of time, as far as work goes, but Jim wants me to go. They're giving us a flat, which means self-catering, and you know how he gets if he has to boil an egg. And there'll be other playwrights, from other countries, as well, so we'll doubtless have an interesting time. I'm not mad about foreign climes, as you know, I'd much rather stay with my little cat... but at least I'll get to see you, and that's a bonus I didn't expect until next summer. Jim says he can spare me for a couple of weeks. He's up to his eyes with his new draft — I spend most evenings typing for him these days. After all, why should we pay a typist when I can do it better anyway?

Do you have any contacts with or about Professor Ball? He's

a bit of a ladies' man, I hear, and not keen on women scholars, but it would do me a lot of good if I could recruit his support for the J. S. biography. I'm not willing to lie on my back to get his interest, obviously, but if I could get him to lunch, perhaps through a third person, I might be able to engage his involvement. After all, J. S. is a comparatively new field and this material from New York is untouched. Let me know if you know anyone who can help. I met an American student who said he propositioned her after only one seminar. But *they're not all like that*, Meg!

Do write soon. I miss you too.

My love,
Frances

Meg to Frances

7 January

Dear Frances,

Thanks for your letter. How super that you're coming over. Yes, of course you can stay, you know that. Let me know where and when to pick you up.

I found the first part of your letter rather hard to bear. Why do you rebuke me for saying what I think? Especially after I told you how much I'd thought about your friendship during that long time when you didn't write — you still haven't said why it was such a long time and you evaded my interpretation of your silence. Is that what you keep calling my 'intensity'? You make me feel as if my commitment to our friendship is actually greater than yours (which I hope is untrue) and that therefore it is my job to do all the thinking about it, while you sit back enjoying your life and denying that relationships have any social meaning. You even accuse me of *taking* something away from you by thinking and talking about it! You say you want to imagine me living my life, and therefore to tell you about the house and Simon and so on, but the living of my life does not only involve what I do and how I react, but, more deeply, what I think and experience. For me, the world holds no interest except for the meaning, or lack of it, that I can find through my own efforts. It is no pleasure for me to think of you cooking and cleaning and writing — I wait for your letters to see what point you are at. But, since you ask, Simon is healthy and active — off to school next year. He's a great source of joy and of intermittent frustration. He's nearly five now and I still have no regrets. As for the house, work and other things, they go on as usual. I'm happy enough and have plenty to do.

I wish we could talk. But soon.

Love,
Meg

P.S. I forgot to say I do know someone who knows John Ball (Professor Balls, they call him) — she's a former star student of his and says that if you can keep him at two arms' length, he's a good teacher and knows everyone who's worth knowing in the field. She said she could arrange a lunch with him and invite you, as you suggested, and to tell you to wear your most dreary wardrobe. And don't interrupt him or challenge his opinion about anything — apparently he gets really turned on by 'aggressive' women. But you have to turn him on a little bit, or he won't be interested in what you're doing. She said her technique was to be very clever about her work but to profess very religious views on everything else. He doesn't try if you're very religious. Are his connections really worth going through all that?   M.

જ

Frances to Meg

20 January

Dear Meg,

Thanks for writing so soon. This will have to be rushed — Jim is pestering me about a draft I haven't finished yet. Mainly to say I'm looking forward to our week together — details about flights etc. on the back of this. Also, can Jim come for three days at the end of May? He's got a chance to see someone useful in Spain, but not till June, and he'd like a few days in London if possible. I shall be back in New York by then (the old lady has got *piles* more stuff!) but I shall be back home by August if you can still make it. Let me know about Jim coming — a card will do.

Professor Balls sounds tricky, but it can't be helped — as your friend said, he knows everyone and is therefore a necessary stepping stone for me. I wonder what the male students would do if they had to cope with it — but that's your territory, isn't it?

Is there something special you would like me to bring for Simon? Let me know. And for you, of course. I can't tell you how much I'm looking forward to being with you again. You are a sort of life-line for me.

Till soon,

Love,
Frances

ॐ

Meg to Frances

2 February

Dear Frances,

Yes, Jim can come.

I know you said you were rushed, but *again* you haven't answered any of my points. Is your 'love' for me so mechanical? or just fragile? I suppose I'm specially disappointed because I had your letter just after a women's meeting at which perfect strangers were able to talk about their sexuality with each other in a much more open way than you and I do, even when we've known each other all this time. One woman said, for example, that she and her male friend *never* engage in sexual intercourse; that they want to explore their sexuality in other ways within their relationship; and they both feel satisfied. I felt really excited by this while she was talking, because it meant that people don't have to remain locked up within the sexual stereotypes society invents. Women need to share this information in order to encourage each other's attempts at experiment and exploration. And I thought how what she and her lover are doing is essentially no different from what I do with my lover and that maybe there's no such thing as 'being a lesbian'. There is only being a woman, irrespective of the sex of one's partner. We ought not to accept an identity based on someone else's anatomy. The penis — I mean, the *symbol* of the penis — ought not to be allowed to divide women from each other. Are you and I, for example, really essentially different? Might it not be an important further stage in our friendship if we did not feel divided, as we have always done in the past, by this barrier of sexuality which may turn out to be artificial?

We have always accepted that the reason we didn't go to bed together was that I was 'lesbian' and you were 'heterosexual', but I wondered, while this woman was describing her experiences, whether that was really some artificially imposed conditioning which ran so deep that neither of us ever questioned it. Why shouldn't we question it? Since we feel very deeply involved with each other — 'love' each other — is it reasonable that we should find each other's bodies repugnant just because one of us doesn't have a penis? Is the penis *of itself* really so essential to you? It isn't for this other woman. I hope at the next meeting that some of the other 'heterosexual' women will talk about all this as well. The woman who spoke is called Amy. I hope you will be able to meet her when you are in London.

Anyway, good luck with your preparations and the journey — and with all those drafts, which I don't envy you. Who types up your own drafts? You, I suppose.

Love,
Meg

Frances to Meg

14 February

Dear Meg,

I hardly know how to answer your letter. I must say it never occurred to me that men and women would do anything else other than sexual intercourse — in the end, I mean. What does this Amy mean?

It's also never occurred to me to want to go to bed with you. I thought it had never occurred to you either. We always said we had a special friendship and that the fact that you were a lesbian and I wasn't, didn't matter. Whoever Amy is, she's put ideas into your head that weren't there before. I must have been right all the time, in spite of all your intellectualisations — feminism is just another name for lesbianism, when it comes down to it. I support women's issues, as you know — abortion, equal pay, all the rest of it — but I don't support the rejection of men as human beings, which it seems to me is what lesbians do. I don't mean anything personal by that — the *idea* of lesbianism. It rather frightens me.

When I think about Jim, I don't specially think of his penis. But I can't imagine feeling about a woman the way I feel about him. My feeling for you is more emotional, more mystical, somehow. Bodies don't come into it. Anyway, let's talk about it when we meet.

Until then, my love
Frances

ॐ

Meg to Amy

15 February

Dear Amy,

I'm sorry we can't meet for another month — I found your contribution to the discussion quite overwhelming and as you said you wouldn't mind if I wrote to you while you're up north, I thought I'd take you up on it and ask you, if you have the time, to tell me more.

You said you and Tim didn't engage in sexual intercourse but that you were constantly exploring your sexualities together. Could you go into some gory detail? I've slept with men a few times, but all my important relationships have been with women. The men certainly wanted a quick screw (or it seemed very quick to me) which left me more or less uninvolved — but I thought I was uninvolved because I was a lesbian and that heterosexual women must enjoy it in the same way as I enjoyed being with a woman. Sex with my women partners was certainly different — emotionally and physically.

I know what women do together, but could you tell me what sort of things you and Tim do? Lesbians are said by orthodox clinicians to indulge in 'mutual masturbation' which means, I suppose, stimulating each other to orgasm by using hands, mouth, thigh or whatever. I've never met a lesbian who used a dildo but many lesbians like to be penetrated either with fingers or with the tongue. Many others don't like penetration specially. Whether one likes it or not, it certainly isn't necessary in order to have an orgasm. When will men catch onto the idea that a woman's sexual organ is her clitoris, not her vagina!

I suppose I should explain that that meeting where we met came at a crucial time for me, a time in which I am having to think again about things I had assumed were clear and settled long ago. On the one hand, I have my relationship with my lover Jan, who was also at the meeting, and on the other, a long-standing friendship with a Canadian called Frances, who is heterosexual. I've loved Frances for years, and she me, but never in a sexual way. It seemed clear that neither of us wanted that. And it seemed clear to me that sex was one thing, and friendship another, and that the two kinds of relationships could co-exist perfectly well. But since I've come into contact with feminism, and specially the whole debate about lesbianism and its political meaning (or message?), my relationship with Frances has somehow run into subtle difficulties which I don't really understand. I keep trying to talk to her about it but she thinks I am inventing problems because of what she calls my feminist 'ideology'. She attacks feminism and, I try to explain to her, she therefore attacks me, while at the same time feeling the love for me that she has always felt and acknowledged. I can't seem to get anywhere discussing all this with Jan. She's never had this kind of intense, non-sexual friendship anyway and doesn't take it terribly seriously — I get the impression that for her my involvement with Frances is a kind of artistic indulgence, a bit of unnecessary icing on the cake.

When I said Frances won't 'talk' about all this, I meant write about it, since because we meet so rarely (she lives in Canada) most of our contact is via letters. She will be in London soon and my ulterior motive in writing to you now is to ask you if you might be willing to meet her and add your presence to a talk with the two of us. My instinct, as well as my understanding of feminism, tells me that the focus of what is happening to my relationships with women I care about has something very particularly to do with sexuality and that that might be a microcosm of the present problem being argued about in the women's movement between lesbian and heterosexual women.

Frances, by the way, is married to a guy called Jim, who is a playwright and a sort of professional egotist. None of her friends like him, but because he is so important to her, I've always thought it my *duty* — as well as my desire to please her — to be friendly towards him. He will be coming too, but not at the same time as she is. Each time she comes to stay, she weeps for a week or so about how he devours her time, her energy and so on and asks me what is going to happen to her. My role is to reassure her that she is important, that life is worth living, all that sort of thing. Then she settles back into her warm, intellectual persona — the person I like so much. She tells me I am her life-line. Recently I am not so happy with these set roles. Somehow it isn't going to be enough for me to go to the theatre and talk about art if we can't get this thing clear about feminism and sexuality, whatever that is.

I don't think I've ever written like this before to a stranger. But then, somehow you don't seem a stranger to me, even though I suppose you are one. I hope very much that you can find time to write back to me.

In sisterhood,
Meg

ଛ

Amy to Meg

19 February

Dear Meg,

I was touched by your letter. Yes, we are strangers, but we are also sisters. I do understand a lot of what you said. Since I became a feminist, I have had two friendships which were very important to me, both with lesbian women. I did sleep with one of them, but we both decided that was not what we really wanted — or not what the friendship really wanted. With the other friend, we tried to talk, as you have tried to talk to your friend Frances, but it wasn't possible. My friend, like yours, was resentful about my involvement with feminism and yet she was a lesbian and I was a heterosexual.

There is something wrong with these words, 'lesbian' and 'heterosexual'. I have begun to think they are only subtle tools of the patriarchy and not women's words at all. After all, patriarchy will not lie down and die just because we have won some abortion rights and the semblance of equal pay. You and I know, even if our friends don't yet, that patriarchy is much more deeply rooted than that. It's a philosophy which moulds the deepest parts of our personalities — so much so that it even feels 'normal' and 'natural'. Nothing is more fundamental to a person's identity than sexuality — one knows that when one is confronted by a transsexual and one doesn't know which pronoun to use about him/her. The first principle of patriarchy is that we divide people into male and female. That has been done to us, and nothing can undo it. The best we can do is to understand the process.

I've talked endlessly about this with Tim, who is motivated (mostly) to throw off his male conditioning. He joined a men's group to explore the possibilities from their side. These men are not quirky. The best analogy I can find for them is the model that is used in an analysis of racism. In a white supremacist society, like ours, white people, whether they like it or not, or choose it or not, are in a position of privilege by comparison with black people. The law may say all people are equal and may enshrine equality of civil rights, opportunities for employment and so on, but the practical experience black people have is that they are not judged on their merits, whatever the law may say. A white person who is 'nice', who believes in individualism, who is liberal and humanist, may repudiate his superiority as much as he or she likes, but the fact of white privilege remains a fact. When that same 'nice' white person applies for a job, he or she will automatically be taken on his or her merits. The black person, by contrast, will not be so treated. The black person will have to prove, either directly or in some unconscious way, that he or she is 'as good' as a white person — in other words, explain away his or her blackness.

Similarly, if we are told about a fight between a white man and black man, our subliminal response is different from our response to hearing about a fight between two white people or between two black people. Our stereotype of the black person becomes superimposed on the incident. It is not possible, because of our social conditioning, to think of the white man and the black man engaged in a conflict, as really equal.

White people who really feel committed to fighting racism and to getting rid of white supremacism, know that it is not enough to be 'nice', liberal-humanist and individualistic. They know they have to put their views into practice by adopting strategies of positive discrimination. It is no use treating black people as equals when it is obvious that, as a group, they are not equal at all. It is much harder for a black person to achieve status, to get a job, to be respected, than it is for a white person. Positive discrimination does not only mean employers recruiting black people. It is much more subtle. It means listening to how black people describe their experiences, listening to their perceptions and world-view, listening to their analysis of racism — and accepting their words as truth. Not saying 'you shouldn't feel like that because. . .' or 'it's not really that bad — look at me — I'm a nice white person'. When one listens to what it really is like for them, one gets a different perspective and a different awareness of oneself and one stops being so smug about one's liberalism and 'niceness'. The point is that a white person, quite irrespective of personality, motivation, inclination, values, or anything else, enjoys the status quo of being 'normal'. Most people, if asked to describe an Englishman or an American, would describe someone who was, among other things, white. The black Englishman or black American therefore becomes deviant from the norm and has to *prove* some sort of normality or identity with the powerful majority.

I've said all that because some anti-sexist men, so I'm told, try to use the same model, translated into the imbalance patriarchy has constructed between the sexes. They see men as privileged and dominant, like white people, and women as suppressed and unequal, like black people. They may be 'nice', liberal-humanist men who believe in individualism, but they are politicised enough to speculate that that is not enough if male power is to be challenged. They know they enjoy status and privilege, even if personally they want to repudiate it. In their group sessions they try to analyse how this privilege works and to become more aware of how unthinkingly all males internalise it.

For example, I suggested once, to Tim, that men should think about being out at night. All the men in turn might describe the last time they had gone out at night — what the purpose was, how they got where they were going (on foot, bus, car, etc.), what they felt about going there, how they went home and at what time, whether anything about any of these circumstances restricted their activity and how often they might go out in the same way again. Then they might go through the whole exercise again, pretending to be female instead of male, to see what sorts of differences being female might make. Then they might realise things about the danger women are in, compared with themselves, all the time, and what a burden it would be to have to plan around that danger as a matter of course.

Another session might be applying for jobs — first in the male role, then thinking of the same experience as it would be for a woman. When they discuss sex in detail, they might use the same technique, trying to see what a particular sexual experience would be like for the woman and using any information their female partners had given them to help their understanding. Putting themselves mentally in the position of their female partners is potentially much more fruitful than thinking up sexual innovations which might encourage the woman to be more 'active' towards them, for example.

The process should be about learning to give priority to women's feelings, women's demands, women's perceptions of how things are for them, so that challenging and repudiating their own sexism means positively and actively making a commitment, intellectual and emotional, to the priority of women's claims. Accepting that the only people who know and understand the experience of oppression are the oppressed themselves, and that saying, from a position of privilege, that one 'understands' what being oppressed must be like is merely superficial, smug and patronising and that no woman worth her feminist consciousness would take any serious notice of such posturing.

Anti-sexism is seriously necessary. Their programme should include the notion of being accountable — being able to service women's needs in preference to their own so that the balance may eventually be restored. This kind of positive discrimination, whether we are thinking about racism or sexism, is a kind of historical corrective. It's like trying to illuminate the way inequalities have been institutionalised to the point where they are just thought 'normal'. By making themselves accountable to women, anti-sexist men would do very obviously things which are not thought 'normal'. Apart from giving practical help to women who sorely need it, this would show less conscious people that all contracts and interactions between women and men need to be re-thought and re-worked.

For example, if women are holding a conference, anti-sexist men should make it a priority to be willing to look after the children. If Tim gets involved in that sort of activity, I challenge his tendency to patronise, his tendency to assume that he is doing a favour to more or less helpless women. I think he should give labour, time and energy where it is long overdue, in the same way that white aid to black societies is seen as some form of partial reparation for the crimes committed by our white forebears. An individual may say he is not responsible for what has happened in the past, and that if it were, or had been, up to him, such things would never have been done and that *he* would never behave like that. Such comments are irrelevant: first, they are totally hypothetical, secondly such things *were* done, and have had effects that still cause suffering, and thirdly we are not able to detach ourselves from history as if we were above the conditions that have created our own society. In that sense we have a responsibility to pay for the mistakes or crimes of our forebears, just as future generations will have to pay for ours.

We are now at a point in history where the refinements of sexism, its vaunting of male privilege and all its perverted workings are being glimpsed by a few people — by feminists and, latterly, by some anti-sexist men. The vision of reality these people have might seem as crazy to the majority as the female suffrage arguments appeared to the majority in the 1890s. Nearly a century later, female suffrage is seen to be quite normal, and the appearance of craziness which the few people of the wider (and correct) vision evoked is now, to us, itself rather crazy. If the legal trappings of female and black emancipation are now 'normal' to us, how inevitable it is that the present feminist vision, held by only a few, will become 'normal' to the generations of the next century. The refinements of sexism, the unconscious exercise of male privilege just now being identified and challenged, will be common knowledge in the future, and the post-patriarchal attitudes of the future will have just as much pity and contempt for our lack of sophistication, for our plain ignorance, as we have for the societies which practised slavery and witch-burning.

Which brings me back to the bedroom. Anti-sexist men are not practising self-denial or pious sacrifice. They are supposed, consciously, to be holding back from the self-gratification they have been taught to expect and by so doing, to be seeking the liberation that comes from discovering what one really feels and really wants. Tim has said, often, that the routine of penetration, ejaculation and falling asleep is boring, limiting, alienating in the end — that the act of sexual intercourse as commonly perceived and practised results in an alienation from his own body — it's too general and de-personalised. In addition, the internalised equation of sex equals penetration equals orgasm equals masculinity equals power equals dominance, and all the rest of it, makes the male limited and oppressive. In other words, the politicised male should learn to see himself from the woman's viewpoint and to accept that what she tells him is the truth — he should take her seriously and not accuse her of being neurotic or aggressive. I think — I hope — that the men intend to work a lot on their sexual conditioning and to come round to seeing that having sex when one feels good with oneself is really the healthiest use of shared sexuality and that a lot of male conditioning unconsciously promotes sex as therapy for any and every occasion, as comfort for feeling bad, as a way of exerting dominance, and as a way of defusing women's own active sexuality.

I could go on, and will if you ask me another time, but there is so much being discussed that I can't get it all down in one letter.

One last thing though — the men still have orgasms, if they want them. Tim says what is important is to learn from women that sex is more than having orgasms and that even without having an orgasm one can feel intimate and emotionally satisfied, just as many Hite report women have described. The difference is that the sexual activity is not goal-oriented. If orgasm happens, that's fine — if not, that's fine as well. Starting from this open-ended position, the men might find a sense of growth, fulfilment and maturity they didn't experience previously and also feel liberated from the expectations of masculinity which have fettered their wider possibilities. Just as women don't want to be treated as sexual objects, anti-sexist men mostly do not want to behave like macho studs, but even when they do, we don't allow it.

In our relationship we struggle to bring together some of the things we have discovered separately from our single-sex groups. We have both agreed that until we can both feel completely comfortable with the *thought*, as well as with the activity, we will not engage in penetration. It is too loaded with expectation and performance-symbolism. It is the arche-typal image of women's oppression by men. And since I do not want to be oppressed, and will not allow Tim to be my oppressor, we don't do it. We touch and stroke a lot; we kiss, fondle, lick, nuzzle, nibble — all the usual things. He rubs my clitoris with his head, with his hand, with his thigh or whatever — just as lesbians do. I straddle his thigh, just as lesbians do. Sometimes he penetrates me with his fingers, if I wish. He does not put his penis inside me anywhere — not in my mouth, my vagina or my behind. This does not mean that he never has an orgasm; he often does. But he says that his orgasm is not as important to him as our mutual pleasure and that an essential part of his liberation — of the liberation of male sexuality — is the overcoming of the tremendous pressure on men to 'come' all the time.

As for me — his penis is as relevant or irrelevant to me as his hands or arms or legs. I should tell you that the reason for *not* having vaginal intercourse is not primarily to avoid pregnancy, as Tim has had a vasectomy. But I know that for a lot of women, avoidance of pregnancy is very important and that many of their men are not yet at the point where they can think objectively about vasectomy.

Different heterosexual couples are at different stages in all this and I don't mean to preach that what Tim and I have been exploring and finding is a sort of new norm. Part of what women's liberation is about — what any liberation is about — is freedom from imposed norms and expectations and provi-sion for the individual of enough information and experience for a genuine *choice* to be made — about what sort of partner, what sort of practice, what sort of aims and values and expec-tations are involved, what sort of people we want to be, and so on. Tim doesn't say all men ought to have vasectomies —

but he does think it should be a considered *choice*. That being reproductive should be positively chosen or positively not chosen. Women, after all, are forced to make this sort of choice. Some women feel, rightly I think, that having to take the pill, risk the dangers of an IUD or, worst of all, to have to cope with the trauma of abortion, just to protect a man's view of his masculinity, is a form of oppression that must be challenged, and the only effective way to challenge it is to refuse vaginal intercourse.

Psychoanalysts would call me, and women like me, lesbian. They would see our unwillingness to agree to vaginal intercourse as a wish to castrate men; and they would probably see our wish for a dominant sexuality of our own as a perversion of normal femininity. Any perversion of 'normal femininity' is, at bottom, classed as lesbianism. I don't agree with them about wanting to castrate, but I would agree that our effort is 'lesbian' — in the sense (deeply important for women) that we are treading the road to our own autonomy with as much passionate ambition as we can muster. It is a source of constant grief, pain, sadness, rage — what you will — that some of the 'lesbians' in the movement have to reject me, reject those like me who are struggling with men on the problem of sexual liberation.

I hope that when we meet we can discuss much of this further, but in the meantime let me say I'd be happy to meet your friend Frances, if you think it might help. Don't give up thinking about all this — it's important.

In sisterhood,
Amy

ॐ

Meg to Amy

23 February

Dear Amy,

I can't thank you enough for writing me such a frank letter. You have succeeded in breaking my isolation. I was beginning to think that I might be alone with some obsession that didn't make sense to anyone except myself. I would so much like to send a copy of your letter to Frances, if you wouldn't mind. Because you are living with a man, she may find points where she can understand you or your point of view better than she can mine. Can I send it to her?

One thing bothers me. If you see yourself, and other heterosexual women, as behaving or feeling as lesbians do, why are you actually with a man? I mean, if the penis is not essential or even specially important to you, I don't quite see why you need to put so much energy into the opposite camp. I don't mean anything personal against Tim (who sounds quite unlike the kinds of men I've been used to!) but I mean, what political meaning can be gained for feminism from what you are doing? I think I understand the political meaning of feminism — the essential independence from men — but I can't see what feminist political meaning can come from a heterosexual couple. It is still the marriage/family/reproduction *image*, if you see what I mean. When you and Tim walk down the street, onlookers see you as just another normal pair. If there is a revolution going on in your bed, how can they know about it?

I hope I don't offend you by saying this; I don't mean it as an attack at all — I'm not a 'lesbian separatist' — I don't think I am, anyway. I live in a house full of women, but I have a son, too. I've heard that some women consider giving up their sons — leaving them — admitting that maleness must lead to patriarchy. I can't face the idea of giving up my son. Is it that you, for example, can't face giving up Tim? Is it relevant whether a woman makes a sexual relationship with a man before or after she comes into contact with feminism?

I am specially interested in your remarks about the symbolism of vaginal intercourse, but how can we change such a deep-seated image? Archetypal, I think you called it. The image itself is so confused, when you think about it. The combination of power, cruelty, dominance, force (penis-as-weapon, rape, etc.) together with creation, reproduction, fruitfulness and love. The combination of all these things in the image of male and female coupling is truly unholy — somehow primitive, 'natural' if you like. Civilization, after all, is built on anti-nature principles. Are we at a point in evolution where we must separate these emotions and functions if we want to survive?

I hope you will have time enough to write back. Meanwhile my greetings.

> In sisterhood,
> Meg

ક્ર

Amy to Meg

26 February

Dear Meg,

Thanks for your letter, which I'll try to answer as fully as I can. But before I do, by all means send a copy of whatever I write to you to your friend Frances, if you think it will help. Part of the political meaning of 'the personal is political' is the publicising of the personal.

I am not offended by your asking why I am with a man. There are some trivial, common-sense anwers, to begin with, like the fact that I was with him before I got involved with feminism. My romantic-plus-lust responses have always been focused on men; perhaps that is merely the result of early conditioning — I don't know. I've always wanted to have a good relationship with a man — and if I have to change the world to have it, then I'll try.

When I met Tim, who had a brain and a sense of refinement, as well as nice eyes and a good body, I fell for him. Such men are rare enough, I know. I'd already been through the usual horrendous experiences with men, including being married to a five-year-old, as many women are. With Tim I had a chance. He was capable of being interested in *me*, as a person. He didn't always treat me as his chattel. He *likes* women — how we feel, what we think. After my initial contacts with feminism, mainly through a consciousness-raising group, he responded to the pressure I put on him to change the dynamics between us. I mean, we both began to see that we were not just separate, individual people even in our own space — we were also cultural products, with a cultural identity — his male, mine female. We wanted to erase that as much as possible. We've worked hard, for years now, at our relationship, trying to get beyond our own conditioning and to find ways of being together that are not oppressive. This is not to say that Tim is either meek or compliant. He fights like hell. But like many women, I just stand firm, stake out my territory, and tell him to change or go. Sure it's depressing — or infuriating — or both. You can't ever really trust a man. And there are good times, but I mostly keep quiet about them — men can get complacent so easily. I believe men *can* change — but only in response to constant and vigilant pressure. They won't and can't change by themselves.

Up to the time I began with Tim and discovered feminism, I had never had a lesbian experience or known any women who were lesbians. Therefore my first introduction to lesbianism meant seeing it as a political act — as the clearest and least ambiguous way of denying power to men. But I could not bring any personal history to the idea. Don't forget I'm over forty; with feminist sex education, my history would have been different, since we all know now that every woman has the potential to relate sexually to other women.

The other 'personal' note I should add is that having become a feminist, and formed deeply important friendships with women, I discovered that I was threatened by the idea of being in a lesbian relationship, because it seemed to offer more intensity than a relationship with a man, and that was a threat to my autonomy. I was afraid of being sucked down into a quicksand of another person's feelings. I haven't quite worked through this yet. It's something to do with the mirroring of myself — complete identification is possible with a woman, because she is like me, and it is not possible with a man — not now, anyway, not at this time in this culture. With a man, I need not negotiate. I can take control, I can

refuse penetration and he can take it or leave it. Stopping
penetration is the first step in breaking the sexual habit/
pattern. In the end, of course, penetration will be available
again — but only as *one option among many*. After all, the
other female primates control when and when not they will
accept penetration. Women want to take that control back to
themselves.

Going back to your question, I think the movement is
forced by reality, ultimately, to find ways of living with men
— making some accommodation. They are half the population
and are not going to disappear overnight. And like you, I have
a son. I refuse to leave him and can't see how I could reject
Tim and at the same time keep my son. What would it mean
to John? That I would love him while he was a little boy, but
not when he became a man? That women are not *capable* of
bringing up sons? That my feminist sisters who are mothers
of daughters have more chance of success than I have? (But
how many daughters of feminists grow up to reject feminism?) Even if I didn't have a son, the human feelings Tim and
I share are real and not to be dismissed on a matter of abstract
principle. That is the way of bigots and sects who end up
denying the importance of all human feelings. I do not want
to end up with an ideology which says sex is only as func-
tional as shitting. And I certainly couldn't go to bed with a
woman in that callous way, substituting principle for feeling.
I know revolutionaries say feelings are bourgeois, decadent
and luxurious, but I can't agree with them. Getting rid of
patriarchy means getting rid of men's *power* over us, not
getting rid of men, or, even worse, getting rid of our own
feelings.

I am not married to Tim, and my son John is not Tim's
biological offspring, though Tim is as much a parent to John
as I am. Nor am I financially dependent on him, but if I had to
be, I would not feel guilty about it, since it is not my fault
that men are able to demand better jobs and money than
women can. If people see us in the street and invest us with
the same image as the conventional boss-man and dependent-
woman, that can only be changed by educating them, by

making them aware of other possibilities. I don't see that my leaving Tim and walking down the street with my arm around a woman will persuade the women looking at me to re-think their own positions. If anything, I can imagine it making them even more secure and entrenched in their patri- archally-based identities. They might feel even more 'differ- ent' from me and unable to identify. That may be part of what is happening with you and your friend Frances. As long as she feels 'different' from you she does not have to take what you say seriously, in the sense of it having anything to do with her.

About vaginal penetration: quite simply, we should think about giving it up. Not participate in this act. Unless we are *deliberately* planning to become pregnant. In this way we can isolate the actual meaning of vaginal intercourse, which is reproduction. We ought to be insisting that reproduction does not 'prove' a person's masculinity any more than it proves a person's femininity — these concepts are now archaic, or should be. Reproduction is only acceptable if it is chosen freely. When men want orgasms, there are plenty of other ways they can have them. Penetrating a woman represents invasion of her body-space and her psychological space as well, just as penetrating *anything* represents invasion. The vagina exists to convey sperm to the womb and babies into the world. It does not exist to give men pleasure or, even worse, pleasure together with a sense of power. They must also learn to be independent; not dependent on shoving into women's vaginas in order to feel good.

Other feminists may still be engaging in vaginal inter- course, but if they are, they are doing so on their own terms and for their own reasons. For me, penetration means the power of the male established over me, and therefore I refuse to allow it. Revolution always embraces an element of puri- tanism, so to speak; in this case, whether or not women have learned to 'enjoy' vaginal intercourse, is not the uppermost question: it is necessary, for our political clarity, that women should first understand the *meaning*, the cultural meaning, of intercourse — for example the image of possession it evokes.

And for another example, the definition of virginity being based on whether or not penetration by the penis has taken place. (Are lesbians virgins?) All this needs to be very, very clear to a woman who engages in vaginal intercourse on her own terms.

Yet although men must, for the moment, 'give up' vaginal intercourse, they can gain from us on all other fronts. They can learn from us about the eroticism of the whole body, about the pleasure of touching the skin, about the importance of atmosphere, about the importance of taking a long time over sexual encounters, about learning to be really vulnerable emotionally — oh, hundreds of things at which women are more expert than they are. When the public finally understands that feminists don't necessarily 'fuck', they will have less rigid images in their minds when they see us walking down the street with our arms around men.

I can see that there are other possibilities; that there may be women stronger in identity than I am, who have learnt how to be the 'fucker' — but as far as I know, that makes men impotent. If the woman seems to be dominant, they lose their erections. But it is essential to deprive men of their power, and if sexuality goes as well — if they can't get erections because women are behaving 'aggressively' — then something is badly wrong with their sexuality. They should explore the reasons for that, rather than bleat about being 'castrated'. If men can learn that sex is *not* taking an orgasm — if they can abandon their drive to be the power-monger (even if only because they are forced to) — then 'fucking' may become possible.

I wonder if you'd be interested in writing to Jane, a lesbian I know up here. I'm sure she wouldn't mind giving her opinion on some of these things. She has been married and is now living in a women's house. I've put her name and address on the back of this letter.

In sisterhood,
Amy

Meg to Frances

3 March

Dear Frances,

Just a last letter before you leave. I'm enclosing a letter to me from Amy, which she said she wouldn't mind my passing on. I thought it better to let her speak for herself. I hope you will meet when you are here.

I didn't mean at all that I'm desperate to go to bed with you. I simply meant that we dismissed the possibility out of fear rather than out of any rational exchange. Don't worry; I'm not going to accost you when you come. I have feelings too. And feminism is *not*, most definitely *not*, another name for lesbianism (which I'm beginning to think doesn't actually exist) — feminism is another name for *independence* from men. It is about rejecting men's *power*. But before you can reject their power, you must first be able to *recognise* it. That is what women need more experienced women to tell them about. You know you are special to me; you know how much I value your fine intellect, your refinement of feeling, your friendship for me. But you must admit feminism is not something you really know much about — you have just rejected it on subjective grounds because it didn't 'appeal' to you. People say the same things about politics, but they still vote. Isn't your intellectual conscience troubled just a bit by your own prejudice? Are you afraid of offending Jim?

Anyway, lots of luck with your preparations. And lots of excitement in me with the prospect of seeing you soon.

Love,
Meg

ह▰

Meg to Jane

3 March

Dear Jane,

I hope you won't mind my writing to you. I got your address from Amy, who said that it would be okay for me to ask your opinion on some things we've been writing to each other about. I'm a lesbian, never been married, with a son whom I planned and I live in a house with women, but not a 'women's house'. (No men have ever actually asked to come and live here.) I think I'd be described in some quarters as a bourgeois feminist intellectual with a lesbian past which just 'happened naturally', long before I ever heard of feminism. What I know about you is that you were married, now say you're a lesbian and live in a women's house.

I want to ask you, if I may, about your transition from marriage to lesbianism — whether it happened 'naturally' or as a result of political conviction. And in either case, what feelings were involved. And what your present position is about men — about sleeping with them, living with them, trying to influence them, working with them — and so on. When I phoned Amy recently, she said you'd done a really interesting paper (not all of which she agreed with) on some of this. I'd so much appreciate knowing your ideas — I can't very often meet other women, owing to domestic arrangements and money-earning. Do write if you have time.

> In sisterhood,
> Meg

P.S. Amy said you wrote poems: so do I, so am sending you my slim vol. Address on the inside cover.

ॐ

Jane to Meg

5 March

Dear Meg,

Thank you for your letter. Let me say straight away, so there will be no ambiguity or pussy-footing around, that 'bourgeois feminist intellectuals' need to be radicalised if the movement is not going to lose all its teeth and turn into an ineffectual geriatric. Revolutions are not won with sentiment. Sons must be given up. Abandoned. Brought up by men. There are two reasons for this: (a) men need to be forced to parent, since they would never do it, given a choice and why should women do it (b) more importantly, sons grow up to be men, to be patriarchs, to carry on the tradition of oppressing women. Our energy is needed for ourselves and for our daughters — not one ounce of it should be spent on men.

I hate men. Let me make that as clear as possible. They have not (yet) raped my body, but they have raped my earth, my possibilities and my feelings. I wasted my youth on the torture of getting and keeping 'boy friends' (who were not friends at all) and I wasted my twenties on what people call a happy marriage (which means making a man happy). Now I want to *use* my thirties, for me, and for women. I have no children but intend to have a daughter; if I become pregnant with a son, I shall abort it. There is no other way. Men are genetically disposed to aggression, egotism, violence and power-seeking, however 'nice' some of them appear. The nice ones are simply more subtle about getting what they want. I know. I was married to a 'nice' man. When I wanted more time for my own things, after discovering feminism, he couldn't stand it. He called my feminist friends 'filthy lesbians'. And then wanted to have sex with me! As long as I was willing to be his 'wife' (he loved that word) and keep the house running smoothly and arrange the social life and write the letters he didn't have time for and look after family birthday presents and cards (*his* family as well as my own!) and so on and so on, it was all fine. He gave me enough money (but he *gave* it — it wasn't my *right*), was 'nice' to me in bed (i.e. not violent, just unaware that I might have sexual feelings too, and that they might be different from his) and talked to me about his work, what he was reading, and so on. 'Nice' little boys grow up to be 'nice' men like my ex-husband.

Any collaboration with men, except as a means to lessen their hold on money and power, is out for women. If necessary, because they are too strong for us at the moment, we must withdraw from them, live only with women, and refuse to work for them. I don't mind taking their money, through the avenue of the state, because it is not my doing that the only jobs available for me are working for men, where they get the most money and glory and I get the most shit. I want to work with women, or for a woman if she is not in turn working for a man. If such a job arises, I shall grab it. In the meantime, I live with my sisters in a slum, donated contemptuously by the local council for misfits like us, so we will do no harm squatting. You will call me mad, I know. Women like you see us as neurotic, extremist, fanatical, even psychotic. I understand that. I used to think the same way. But I am not mad at all, or at least, only as mad as this fucked-up patriarchy we live in has made me. They thought black people were mad, too, for not being grateful for hand-outs. Our time is not yet. But it's coming. We have the power of reproduction, after all. When enough of us refuse to bear boys, the men will have to listen to us. Meanwhile we wait and work and help each other.

You asked about my 'transition' to lesbianism. For me it was an awakening. I found sexual contact with women amazing — my sexuality unfolded, developed, became creative and integrated — I felt free for the first time. I'm not saying relationships with women are all bliss — there are conflicts I had never imagined — but the relationships are honest and, above all, equal. Any power we might try and exert is recognised and rejected. We are not fixed into roles. We all have to cook and clean and shop and take responsibility. We all know what it is to be exhausted after a day of housework. We can share our problems and know that they are considered important. Life with women has its problems, but it is stimulating and liberating. There is no place for men here. They are too backward, too egotistic — we would spend too much time, if a man came, nurturing his threatened ego. We don't need to be mothers to men. Let them mother each other. We've done it for long enough.

Amy, as you will know, doesn't agree with me. She says we have a fatalistic, or 'biologically deterministic', view of male human beings which is not based on proper evidence. She means genetic/environmental evidence, sociological surveys and all that. I don't think so. Our history, and the state of our society, are all the evidence an intelligent woman needs. And even the terms for research are patriarchal. I wouldn't trust its conclusions, because I don't trust its assumptions. From birth, men are trained to exploit, oppress and destroy, either overtly or covertly. A little man might 'only' destroy one woman's identity and autonomy, and that may be thought totally insignificant by our society. But it matters to me. I want no part of that.

Feminism to me means devoting all one's strength, energy, love and work to women. That can't be done without withdrawing from the patriarchy as completely as possible. All we need from men is their sperm, well, half their sperm − the female half. As for the rest of their 'humanity', they can crucify each other with it, for all I care. There are women who need us more.

> In sisterhood,
> Jane

&

Meg to Jane

8 March

Dear Jane,

Whew, what a letter! You don't pull your punches, do you? I'm grateful for your honesty but a bit stunned by what I am meant to do with it. I am afraid to say I hate men, having been accused of it all my life because I was a lesbian. Anyway, I don't even know if it's true. I don't hate my son. I certainly hate patriarchy. So does Amy, for example. For me, it is emotionally impossible to abandon my son. Apart from that, it is intellectually indefensible to me − I wanted him born; he had no choice. How can I love him and then leave him on a matter of principle he is far too young to understand? Why should I reject him just because he has a penis? And anyway, what man is going to bring him up? His biological father is, to use your own thoughts, only someone from whom I wanted the sperm and had no relationship with. There are no men to

bring him up. He would be taken by the State, since I am
unmarried, and put into a home or given foster parents, and
be brought up by another woman or women. I'm sorry, it does
seem to me mad.

And even if he didn't exist yet, if I were still pregnant, and
could have found out what sex my baby was (which I couldn't
have found out just by asking — those tests are only given to
mothers with hereditary diseases in the family or in cases of
suspected mongolism or other deformities, none of which
conditions applied to me) — even then, if I knew it was a boy,
I could *not* have faced an abortion. I've experienced a mis-
carriage already, which was the most difficult and depressing
experience of my life — the idea of causing myself that misery
on purpose is inconceivable. Have you ever been pregnant
with a wanted child? Do you really know what you are
talking about? I'm sorry to be aggressive, but what you pro-
pose seems so destructive of all the things that are important
to me, destructive of part of my *womanhood*, which feminism ought, surely, to be protecting.

I can't see, either, that such a strategy is at all practical;
even if two or three thousand women lived as you suggest, it
would not threaten any of the structures we are trying to get
rid of. Surely we have to recruit men as well; surely women
like Amy are in the front line by doing that. I quite see that
having nothing to do with men might be personally good and
liberating — and I see that you have very strong negative
feelings about your ex-husband (as other women have about
their fathers, brothers, bosses or whatever) — but is that a
reasonable basis for a *political* strategy? When people look at
you in your women's house, or me in my house full of
women, knowing that we each sleep with a woman as well,
can they see any essential difference between us? I think that
the fact that men don't *want* to live in my house is itself
significant. They probably wouldn't want to live in your
house either. It's autonomous *women* they don't like,
whether they're lesbians or not, or feminists or not.

I understand what you mean about not wanting to 'educate'

a male newcomer — I wouldn't want to either. Yes, too exhausting. One needs the motivation of personal *feelings*, as I have for my son, or Amy has for her lover. Did you never want to spend that sort of energy on your ex-husband, when you were still fond of him? How can human affection be got rid of? and *should* it even be got rid of?

Even being a lesbian doesn't mean I can like all women, or that I can dislike all men. Some personal elements have to be taken into account, surely. I don't mind being radicalised if I can see why and what sort of result will come about which will be better than what we have now. If you tell 'the public' about your marriage, they will just write you off as a woman soured by a bad relationship, just as they write me off by saying I had a bad relationship with my father. Where does that get us?

You will probably find me too hopeless a case to want to answer this, but I hope you *will* write back. Much as your ideas threaten all of mine, I want to consider them properly and to reject them, if I must, or accept them, for good reasons, not out of fear.

In sisterhood,
Meg

ॐ

Frances to Meg

10 March

Dear Meg,

Thank you for your letter and the copy of Amy's letter to you. At first I was angry that you had discussed our friendship with a perfect stranger — but then I thought, oh hell, what am I getting so uptight about? I know you're bothered by this 'conflict' between us, even though I'm not, and in all the years we've known each other, you've never betrayed me, never not told me the truth, never not listened to me when I had problems, never not taken me seriously. So I thought, perhaps I'm being a bit of a cow, not taking you seriously. God, you don't ask very often. And I'm influenced by the thought of seeing you soon — the warmth of it. You are the only one who knows my mind. I feel safe with you.

Your friend Amy doesn't sound so bad. I was alarmed to start with, when I read her letter, because I'd never heard of that before, never even thought of it — not having intercourse, I mean. But I still can't imagine having sex without a full cunt, if you understand me. Even Germaine Greer said that, as I remember. And I still can't quite see *why* I shouldn't — all that stuff about the symbolism, I mean. I don't *feel* oppressed. Surely that's important?

Anyway, it's all very hypothetical — Jim would never stand for it, not in a million years. You know how he hates discussing anything like that. When we got married (which was my demand, not his — I said I wasn't willing to put up with the notoriety of being his mistress) — he said he'd marry me on three conditions: that there would be no 'wedding' (dressing up, party, etc.), that I would support myself, and that there would be no children. I agreed. I take the pill but I'm getting more and more unhappy about it and am thinking of having a sterilisation. He won't discuss any of it — says it's my decision. I would have liked a baby — you know that — but those were his conditions and I accepted them and I don't see how I can go back on the contract now. I've kept my part. He's never even paid for a cup of coffee for me in a restaurant. I can't *imagine* asking him now, after all this time, to give up intercourse. And as I said before, I can't even see why I should. It doesn't feel right.

Perhaps I'm just dreadfully old-fashioned, but I've never wanted to be an adventurer, except in my work. You know that too. You *do* know me, Meg. Please don't put the sort of pressure on me that you know I can't stand. You're the only one I've got left; I can't seem to talk to Mum any more, and all the people here are Jim's friends. He's so much more gregarious than I am. They're nice enough, but not 'my' people. I need you, Meg. Please be there.

The packing is all finished, thank God, and the drafts all

typed and the cat arranged for and most of the goodbyes said.
Now for the journey, which always makes me want to roll up
in an unconscious heap and get there without knowing about
it. But the thought of you at the other end is sustaining
enough.

Till very soon,
Frances

 క≫

Meg to Amy

11 March

Dear Amy,
    Thanks for your letter which I'm sorry to have taken so
long over — I've been chewing on it. I wrote to Jane and had a
letter straight back — a bullet, rather — right between the
eyes. Being a lesbian is one thing — I've grown up with that
— if it ever was a choice, it was a very dimly perceived one.
But to give up my son — that is quite another thing. I didn't
'dimly' choose to be pregnant — I planned it and wanted it,
knowing all the time that the baby would be one sex or the
other. That wasn't important — what was important was to
have a live, healthy baby. How can I stop being intimidated
by women like Jane? How can I not hate her? What sort of
sisterhood can we all have?
    At the conference last weekend, there were three groups of
children: one run by men, one run by women, and one run by
women for girls only. I suppose that's some kind of democ-
racy, to have such a choice (well, a choice of two out of three
for me!) but what a muddle of ideology it is.... One lot of
women refuse to let men anywhere near their children;
another lot insist that *only* men should mind the children, so
that the women, for a change, can go to their conference and
do what *they* want. Yet a third lot of women refuse to have
their *daughters* near any member of the male sex. Amy, isn't
this the kind of nonsense that brings us into disrepute? Or are
we — you and I — simply rationalising the choices we made

in some state of preconsciousness, and really the way forward is to follow Jane's path? Let me know what you think.

In 'sisterhood' (?)
Meg

ह•

Jane to Amy

11 March

Dear Amy,

Just a note to say I can't meet you on Monday — I'm sorry about it but we've got a sudden crisis in our house and I must stay in for the next few days. The hardest thing about self-help is the time it takes.

I had a letter from your friend Meg, which I've answered. Every time I hear of a woman bringing up sons, I feel depressed — in a way more depressed than when I face women living with men. The energy being devoted to these boys is so much more intense, and the loss to our freedom so much greater. It is so important, so tactically necessary, for women to withdraw from the male sex. We need to build up our resources, to get strong, to develop the sort of confidence the patriarchy has given to men. But also we need to show the men that they must take us seriously. Until we stop — absolutely stop — looking after them and providing all the crutches we have always provided, they will never face what we have faced. I doubt, actually, if they ever could. There seems to me to be no evidence, either genetic or historical, which presents men as anything other than innately aggressive, dominating and destructive. Until evolution, or revolution, can find a way to reduce their levels of testosterone, I can't see any way in which women can live with them without the women becoming damaged. Don't you admit you've been damaged yourself? Why, Amy, can't we free *our* sisterhood from the shadow of men? Why must we even waste our energies *talking* about them?

In sisterhood,
Jane

Amy to Jane

15 March

Thanks for your note. Sorry not to see you on Monday.

I don't share your despair about 'wasting time' on men. Men, after all, are the reason and focus for patriarchy. We have to learn some form of co-existence. We have to learn, too, some methods of containment. Don't you see, even from your own argument (which I don't agree with, by the way) about male aggression, that if we just leave them alone, if we just ignore what they do, they'll become even more violent and destroy us even more effectively. Yes, I've been damaged. We all have. But I refuse to hide in a corner and lick my wounds. All scars can heal, in time, and with women's support. And not every individual embodies all the attributes of patriarchy. There *are* men's groups against sexism, Jane. You never say anything about that. And there are, on the other hand, daughters of feminists who reject everything we stand for. You don't say anything about them either. It's not so black-and-white *simple*, for God's sake! We need to support each other — all of us — in our life-styles.

Your idea about testosterone is interesting. I hadn't thought about it before. I think you're right. That's the male hormone responsible for men having stronger muscles, isn't it? which, I agree, we certainly don't need any more. We don't need anyone to cleave a lion's jaw with brute strength. We don't need brute strength.

I read a piece in the press about athletes taking testosterone — both male and female athletes. It must, it appears, increase both strength and aggression. What if our infant males could be somehow treated so that they produced less of it? Is it male *bodies* you want to expunge from the earth? or is it male *power*? What *I* want to be rid of is male *power*, and in my tiny living-cell, I have a chance to do that. If we all did that, it would make a difference. Not be a 'waste of energy'.

The central myth we must get rid of is that of rape. It must have no place in human society. It must cease to exist, cease to be even imaginable. I don't see how that can be achieved by withdrawal. If anything, withdrawal could increase the possibility. What they can't have by consensus, they may take by force. It is *necessary* to re-educate them. And to re-educate women so that they will psychologically refuse to believe that rape can sometimes be justified. All the rapes we suffer daily — the mental, social and political raping of women by men — will not cease before the central physical fact is made to cease. Physical rape is the phallocentric image of all our oppression. Stand firm, Jane, don't run away.

You mentioned a crisis in your house. Can I help? I'm free three evenings a week at the moment, and all day Friday (apart from letter-writing!!)

> In sisterhood,
> Amy

ও

Amy to Meg

18 March

Dear Meg,

My letter-writing day at last! What a week. Tim phoned up saying my son has mumps, so there I was with the perpetual female schizophrenia again: do I attend to my son (duty, love, guilt, responsibility, etc.) or do I attend to my women's work here (duty, love, guilt, responsibility, etc.)???? Sartre wrote that when there is a choice between right and right and it's only possible to do one, then afterwards one can never say one would have done the thing left *if*. . . . So I have 'neglected' my son (who is not neglected at all being in Tim's hands!) and got exhausted from feeling guilty. I'm a bad mother for not putting my child first and I'm a good mother for not making him totally dependent on me and giving him other strings to his emotional bow.

I've just written to Jane. Yes, there is a personal history involved in her rejection of all males — but if we psychoanalysed everyone in the movement, we would find personal derivations in each case, undoubtedly. So what? We are in a *political* struggle. All people are personally motivated, whatever they're doing or fighting for. The important thing is to struggle with what we have against the evil we know. Abstract personality models are just that — abstract. Jane's position *is* a position, whatever her private reasons for holding it. So is mine. Yes, I'm sure we all rationalise. It's the *positions* that are important — what is tactically correct and what is morally right. It's a cul-de-sac to abuse each other's private feelings and motivations. I oppose Jane because I think her tactical position is not likely to succeed. And I am morally justified in my own eyes for staying with my two particular males because of my fondness for them and my conviction that it is not biological maleness, in itself, that is responsible for our oppression.

Jane suggested something about lowering testosterone levels. I've been thinking about this, testing it on myself; e.g., when my son was born, could I have agreed to someone injecting him or whatever in order to ensure minimal testosterone production, knowing he would therefore be a less 'masculine' man? Would it be abusing my power? Would it be the obverse of those obscene men performing clitoridectomies on helpless girls? I don't know. It's hypothetical, of course. But I did discover in myself (which I'm ashamed of, after all this time) a taboo or an inhibition or what you will that made the male genitalia somehow more sacrosanct, more inviolate, than the female. The possibility of being accused of castrating a male was somehow especially frightening — I would be somehow *particularly* monstrous. Do we, (or should I say I), therefore, unconsciously support the rape myth — the worship of the penis? What do you think about this?

> Love to you,
> Amy

ॐ

Meg to Amy

5 April

Dear Amy,

Joy! Frances is here. Long days and nights spent in endless talking, endless affection, endless caressing with eyes. When my heart is so engaged, my flesh is somehow irrelevant. Nevertheless, I've kept off anything feminist, but only half-deliberately. There's been so much to catch up on.

Thanks for your letter. I know what you mean about the schizophrenia. Ever since Frances arrived I've been suffering myself. Simon is so jealous of my talking to her — and I do choose to talk to her, and to 'neglect' him. Like your son, he has other relationships that are important to him, and he must learn, especially being a boy, that I have other relationships that are important to me. Still, to your list of love-guilt-duty-responsibility I'd add another one — rage. Rage that I have been conditioned to feel the guilt in the first place and am still unable to shake it off. But I fight it. I go on talking.

I must say I've thought about the testosterone thing before but was afraid to mention it to anyone. It's a relief to hear you talk about your 'penis taboo'. I'm a lesbian from way back and therefore have the taboo, or whatever it is, a thousandfold more than straight women must have it. I've always been accused of being a man-hater, which means (unconsciously, everyone means) that I'm supposed to want to castrate men because I hate and fear the penis. I almost half believe it myself. I had this set of feelings when I was advised to have my son circumcised. They didn't say it was really essential. Just a good idea. I went through all this thing: if it has to be done, it will be more traumatic for him later, so better do it now. But am I unconsciously just wanting to maim him, when he can't fight me back? What are my motives? I admit I find the sight of uncircumcised men ugly. Is that aesthetic or conditioned or what? Is it even relevant? And so on. In the end, I decided to have it done. For me the testosterone question would be like that, only more so. But it can't be done, can it? I haven't heard of any research on that. Since the medical profession is run by men, I can't imagine the possibility anyway.

I admit I don't like adult penises much, especially on adolescent boys, who seem to have enormous ones (does the penis develop more quickly than the rest of a man?) — I'm threatened by the sight — yes, afraid (and men like women to be afraid). I know I'm not even meant to look at them, but I have to, like poking at a toothache. I don't think a clitoris is specially beautiful either, but it isn't pushed at my eyes. The penis certainly represents, *embodies*, power for me, brute force. If it didn't, my reactions would be different. Is the difference between us (the 'private' difference) simply that I am more afraid than you are? I never believe pornography which proclaims the tenderness of the penis as a love-object, even when it's written by a woman. When my son is a man, perhaps I will have a more integrated view. I don't know. But without the penis, they couldn't rape us. Are you saying that without testosterone they *wouldn't* rape us? (less testosterone, I mean). Did you know, for example, that it's the penis that gets ordained by the Catholic Church? If a man is a eunuch he can't be ordained. And that's why women can't be ordained.

Now that I am in my thirties I would so much like to be told that my feelings have tapped a true historically validated instinct for autonomy and against subjection rather than the old stuff of being neurotic, fixated, damaged and so on. I certainly had a brute of a father. But so did many straight women. Slowly and painfully I begin to see that it's been my independence of mind or will that has directed my development and that when women like Jane are supported in their search for independence by other women they are gradually confident enough to take the path I have always taken. But what about you? Are you not yet as independent as we are? Is your fear of lesbian closeness a mirror of my fear of male brutality, each basically being a defence against the loss of autonomy, of independence? I want to be free; if not from fear, at least from brutality.

You'll be back in London next week, I've worked out. Can you come round one evening, say Wednesday, and meet Frances? I'd so much like you to. Meanwhile my love,

> In sisterhood,
> Meg

Jane to Meg

9 April

Dear Meg,

I wanted to answer your letter while I was still in the white heat of it, and then I thought better of it, and anyway we had a bit of a crisis here and I didn't have any time for myself. Your letter aroused all sorts of things in me, roused up all my past, challenged all my hopes — I felt sad, angry, depressed — oh, lots of things. But I want to sort some of them out, make friends with you somehow. I can't bear the thought of the women like you being lost. We need you. We need every woman. I hardly know where to start. It's exciting, and inhibiting, when I've never seen your face or heard your voice to have to write to you in such a fierce way But feminism is fierce. It should be fierce. We've got a revolution to win.

You attack me on the grounds of my personal feelings; ask whether I understand the feelings of maternity, whether I'm soured by my marriage, and so on. I reject all that. I reject being in love — the idea of it. I reject anything and everything that smacks of past conditioning. If that's extremism, I don't mind — extremism is necessary to clarify things, to get free. Of course I have feelings — it's patronising of you to imagine I haven't, or that my feelings don't matter to me. *But feelings are not the most important thing.* Change is not brought about by personal feelings. Feminism is the first focus for change that preaches the *politicisation* of personal feelings. Have you not yet discovered that you can direct your feelings with your head? That you can love where you ought to love? That loving what you ought not to love is a sickness, a decadence bringing nothing but misery? Even Christ told people to leave everyone, even those who were closest. We have to put our energy where it will be most productive, and that is why women should be our first priority. The whole question of motherhood is vexed anyway for feminists. How can any woman shake off the expectations of the role? Show our daughters a new way, provide a new model?

Look, you're a lesbian. What does that mean? Surely that you've always lived in defiance, however covert, of male power over your body, in defiance of male possession. You have lived independently from men, except where it was impossible, because they have most of the money, run most of the jobs, and so on. You've been like one of the blacks, except that your slave status wasn't obvious like a black skin. Do black people want to collude with their oppressors? How *can* you even contemplate breeding yet another patriarch? If you could only explain that. How can you?

I want a daughter. I shall have a daughter. And she will be a feminist. We will find ways of handing on our new culture, embattled though we are. No son shall take life from me. Your feelings are a weakness; they weaken our movement; they hurt us. You hurt me by what you say. There is no way you can make sure your son is not going to be another male boss. It's in his chemistry to be so, and everything around him will reinforce that image of himself, whatever you say or do. Can't you see that?

We've just had a woman in our house suffering the most incredible trauma because her son has been had up for beating his wife. This sister has been distraught. We've had police here, bullying her, and us, because he's asked to see her and she won't go and the psychiatrist says she must go if she cares about her son's rehabilitation. She weeps and suffers about what she did wrong. We try and tell her it isn't her fault, whatever these shit male psychiatrists say, who blame everything onto women, onto wives who don't give their husbands what they want, or onto mothers who dominate their sons. We're fed up. We want out. We want the right not to speak to these people. We demand not to be held responsible for acts of violence done by men. She doesn't want to see her son. She's upset even by the thought of him. She says he's always been a basher. Ever since he was a little boy. They're all like that underneath. Who makes war? Who fights in the streets? Who rapes women? Who invents sports like boxing, wrestling, shooting and so on? Who glorifies the exercise of brute power? Is it women? Was it ever women? *What are you breeding*, Meg? Think about it, please.

It's easier to shout at you, somehow, than to shout at Amy. You're still words on a page, a name, a woman I don't know. Of course I have feelings. The more I know you, the softer I'll get. I wish it were not so — we can't afford that sort of weakness. But I want to persuade you. I want you on our side. I want the revolution now, in every house, in every bedroom.

In sisterhood,
Jane

୫

Meg to Jane

11 April

Dear Jane,

I don't mind your shouting at me but it's no good. I love my son, I chose to bear him, and that's it, whatever any of you say. The important thing for me is whether that means you and your women are going to reject me and Amy and the rest of us, or not. Or whether we're going to reject you. Whether there are going to be two women's movements, God help us. Those who want to change men, and those who want to withdraw from them. But that would be just another way of allowing men to ruin the movement. Can't you bear with me, compromise a little?

Apart from my son, and apart from a split in the movement happening in my head, there is a third thing. I have a friend staying with me at the moment — her name is Frances — and she is immensely important to me, has been for years. We are not lovers. But we love each other. She is afraid of feminism — says it's just another name for lesbianism — but is an instinctive feminist, somehow. She is also married and afraid of losing her marriage if she becomes too influenced. People like Frances matter too; they have hopes and fears too. I can't desert her either, and I don't want to. None of it is as simple for me as it seems to be for you. (I don't mean emotionally simple, easy to do — and I do *not* mean to patronise you — I

mean conceptually clear.) I would have to abandon everybody
who is important to me. I know what Christ said. But feminism isn't a religion. And I'm not a mystic. I don't want to
build a new Jerusalem, or even stumble across one. Perhaps
I'm more of a pragmatist.

> In sisterhood,
> Meg

ح

Amy to Meg

> 12 April

Dear Meg,

Wednesday's fine. Look forward to seeing you, and meeting
Frances. John's mumps are just about vanished, thank God, so
I'll be more-or-less mobile as usual. Tim's given me the car for
the week so I'll get most of my work done without too much
hassle. I've been busy with a friend of mine's book. We're
printing it ourselves; the straight publishers said it was too
political and wouldn't sell. Mad. We've got five hundred
copies ordered for it already.

Jane is quite put out by you — or turned on by you —
reacting anyway. More than she does to me. I've known of her
on and off for ages and the argument between us has probably
softened up after what must be weeks of talk. The debate
itself has been going on for years now, but lately it seems
more crucial. What we have to do — somehow — is change
our sexuality itself. Everything about it. Maybe I've been
wrong. Maybe I'll end up having to go to bed with Jane (or
whoever) to prove a point. I hope not.

Some political lesbians in the States are now aborting all
boys. I'd rather make all women stop having any children at
all than have to agree with that.

See you Wednesday,

> Sisterly love,
> Amy

ح

Amy to Frances

20 April

Dear Frances,

I so much enjoyed meeting you — was surprised, in fact, by how much. I sometimes give way to a sort of dread of meeting 'apolitical' women. When one has worked so hard on oneself and has understood so well why things are like they are for women, there can be something truly awful about contact with women who are not in the same space and who still insist that everything is all right with the world except the Bomb, or that everything that goes wrong for them is simply a result of their own personal disorder. I think I had that sort of expectation, which Meg must have unconsciously implanted, though she would not mean to in a million years. But you are open and curious and very responsive to all that we talked about.

It was only the subject of marriage, and especially your own, which seemed to elicit the sort of withdrawal I mean. I wonder why that is? Were you aware of it? Do you think there is something dreadful about discussing one's intimate relationships? Hardly anything else is *worth* discussing, since all problems on a large scale are just projections of conflicts we have to put up with on a smaller scale in relationships. You will say that is very Platonic or Socratic — and I know the patriarchs have been busy thinking up sophisticated systems which will void this basic truth — they have their reasons — but it is clear to all the women I know that unless the personal level is recognised and changed, nothing else can be changed. So it is important, very important, to talk about marriage and any sort of relationship with men.

I'd so much like to hear from you. Will you write?

Love,
Amy

Meg to Amy

21 April

Dear Amy,

Just a note. Things hectic. Wanted to thank you for the meeting with Frances. She understood a lot more having heard you. We had a good time together.

Can't write more now. Can't phone. Jim has been here. It was awful. Wish I could see you.

Love,
Meg

જ

Frances to Meg

21 April

Dear Meg,

I've been really busy since I got back — no time to write properly and I didn't want to send one of those polite notes people send to their aunts saying thank you for a lovely time. Now I have a morning for myself and I *do* want to say thank you for a lovely time. It *was* lovely. Full of warmth and interest and the kind of stimulation only you give to me. I felt as if I'd got my bearings again, as if I know again who I am and what I want to do.

You give me such strength — no, not strength exactly — *recognition*. I know I must have said that before, a million times, but nothing else is quite as true. It's as if I'm drowning without knowing it and then you come along and rescue me over and over again. I wonder really what I ever give you? It seems so one-sided.

I want to thank you as well for the chance to meet Amy, who wasn't at all what I expected. She is so gentle and understanding — not at all aggressive or Gorgon-like. What she said about her relationship with Tim is still unimaginable to me, in my context, but it opened my eyes to some possibilities, though how far I'd ever get with Jim in such a way is something I doubt and anyway, I feel I haven't got the kind of strength or endurance needed for such a battle. I'm used to him, and what I really want to invest my effort in is my work. Home is a refuge from the world, which, as you know, I've always been nervous of — I like to think of home as a fortress which protects me from the big bad world outside, and Jim is part of that protection. I know you'll despise me for that, although you would never say so, but that's how it is for me. Nevertheless, it was really good to meet Amy and I will go on admiring what she's doing from the sidelines.

Thanks for having Jim. I hope he didn't land you with the same pile of dirty washing as he did last time. I told him to go to the launderette before he went to you. He's due back tomorrow. I've missed him. Stupid, really, when we've been married so long. I know he never pines for me.

Your friendship is so special to me, Meg. I can't imagine my life without you. I mean, I wouldn't kill myself, but my life would be so much the poorer if you were not part of it. Please always be there.

My love to you,
Frances

ॐ

Frances to Amy

26 April

Dear Amy,

Thanks so much for your letter. I enjoyed meeting you too, and was surprised not to be more intimidated than I was. But I must say I feel wary about discussing the more intimate details of my marriage — especially on paper. Of course I didn't meet Tim, but what you told me seems unimaginable. I wonder why he doesn't feel dominated. I know you said the two of you had discussed it all over and over, but I still find it hard to believe that a man would sacrifice his sexual pleasure because of a principle. I find it hard enough to understand from religious celibates, so if it's done for something as amorphous and non-religious as feminism, then it seems, as I said, unimaginable. I find it hard to talk about sex anyway, even at parties in a superficial way.

Jim was someone I'd known for years and years — yonks in fact — when I was a student. He was older and not a student and had a reputation for being the world's biggest show-off. I thought of him like that as well and used to entertain my friends, including Meg, with stories of his appalling egotism. But when I went abroad for the first time and felt that sickening weight of loneliness and being displaced, I met up with him — he was doing one of his European 'what's going on in the contemporary arts' gigs — and he was so nice to me and somehow so consoling that I saw another side to him. Well, there must have been another side — no one is just a show-off, pure and simple, and certainly not someone who has made some sort of name as an artist.

He'd already had a long-running affair with a friend of mine but that seemed to have finished — I couldn't have gone to bed with him if it hadn't, not even in the state I was in. So we just sort of came together. I felt miles better. I remember thinking, is that all there is to it? Is all I need to get rid of my depression, someone to lie next to? Someone to be nice to me before breakfast? I've always had such trouble, you see, just managing to live.

I used to say to Meg that being me felt like being behind a window, looking out, and seeing life walking past the window. Life was something that happened to other people. Meg was always so positive — I think she's the most positive person I've ever known, apart from Jim. She used to talk to me and listen for hours until I couldn't understand what was in it for her. She was always much more able to express her feelings than I was, or more able to have the feelings in the first place, perhaps, but as much as her love for me has been fierce and open, mine has been equally strong, but more reticent and hidden. I'm afraid of telling her how much she means to me — but I'm not really sure why. I'm not saying I couldn't live without knowing her, but if I had to do without her, my life would be incredibly the poorer.

I don't know if I'm making any sense. This all seems so garbled. I don't know what it has to do with sex, or, for that matter, what it has to do with feminism, but I wanted to answer your letter and perhaps increase my tiny circle of friends. I don't seem to make friends easily — part of always looking out the window, I suppose — but it did seem to be easy for us to talk to each other, so do keep writing if you'd like to.

Best wishes,
Frances

ॐ

Amy to Frances

1 May

Dear Frances,

Good to have your letter. And no, it didn't seem garbled. It's what I was trying to say to you about the stuff of theory depending absolutely on the integrity of one's experiences. As for your questions regarding my relationship with Tim, I can tell you it hasn't been easy or obvious for either of us. It isn't, you see, a question of his 'giving up' his sexual pleasure in a sacrificial sort of way — not at all. We discussed the politics of penetration over a long period and came to the conclusion that it was invasive and dominating over the woman simply because it cannot yet be freed from the cultural image it carried for us all — that for the man to get it up and get it in is a 'real' fuck, and any other sort of sexual sharing is somehow beside the point.

The only time such action is actually necessary is when two people intend to reproduce. The Church and other instruments of patriarchy have always said that the only purpose for sex was procreation — and that means first of all that the woman's pleasure is immaterial, since you don't have to have an orgasm in order to become pregnant. Secondly, it means that there is no other possible reason for mating, which cuts out all forms of polygamy and all homosexual partnerships. The whole sexual hierarchy is derived from the cultural input of that particular image. All else flows from it — the passivity of the female, the 'rights' of the male, including his 'property' rights, the potential for rape, the supremacy of the male sex over the female sex in all other things *outside* the bedroom (explain *that*, for starters!) and so on.

So Tim and I agreed that the only way we could ever begin to have a relationship which had a chance of being equally balanced would be to begin as sexual equals. Without penetration we have more chance of starting from an autonomous base and we can both begin without preconditioned expectations of what is going to happen and why. A man, after all, does not need a woman's vagina in order to have an orgasm. So why should he think that he does? Isn't it that he has been *taught* to expect it? And isn't it that the woman has been *taught* that he will expect it? Did you ever go out with a male, man or boy, who didn't expect to penetrate you if you both decided to become sexually involved? Were you not constantly pestered about your 'virginity', while you had it? Did the male not behave as if 'nothing had happened' if you did *not* have penetration? Haven't you wondered why women are divided into those who are 'virgins' and those who are not? What woman, for God's sake, would ever think up a concept like 'virginity' to categorise herself with? *Men* care about 'virginity' — it doesn't mean a stuff to women. Even after women have 'given in', they often as not report a huge feeling of letdown — something along the lines of 'is that all it is?' or 'why do they make such a fuss about it?' Why indeed?

Well, that was a paragraph full of questions. I'm sorry to seem aggressive, but I want to tell you, in whatever way I can, that feminism is about all these things and that all the things you think are personal and unique to you also have a general and therefore *political* meaning. I wanted to comment also on what you have said about Meg. I haven't known her all that long, but I know her well enough to see what a passionate nature she has and to know, too, how important your friendship is for her. I wondered if it was equally returned, I must admit, but after seeing you together and feeling the warmth between you, it was obvious — you don't have to explain about being more reticent. Most people are probably more reticent than Meg.

Do write soon,

Love and sisterhood,
Amy

ह

Frances to Amy

6 May

Dear Amy,

Thanks for your letter. Some of your questions are a bit mind-boggling — or emotion-boggling, I should say. It's funny you should bring up that business about virginity. At least that's something I can agree about and I understand everything you say about it. I used to have awful depressions all through my student days — I still do, except there isn't so much empty time to have them in as there was then.

Anyway, I had a friend who was much more active than I was, wore exotic clothes, went to all-night parties — that sort of thing. She said to me that there were three things to try — and that one of them must work. They were priest, psychiatrist and lover. I did the lot. The priest didn't work, because I found out I could only have the right set of feelings in the church when there was old music playing — Renaissance *a capella* singing and so on. When the music wasn't there I didn't feel a thing, so I concluded that my religious responses were merely to music and not to God. Then I tried the therapist — that didn't work either — he couldn't think of anything that might be wrong with me that he could fix — he just told me to have a more positive attitude and that life was really fun if you looked at things the right way. That left the lover. So when a guy picked me up at a party and suggested I went home with him, I agreed, since that was my last hope. I remember lying in the bed and looking up at the wall thinking I was really just a fly on that wall, watching what was happening. It wasn't happening to me at all. I didn't feel a thing. I remember thinking 'is this all there is to it?' and remember, as well, that the best part of it was going home in the morning. I think it was the most nothing experience I ever had in my life and the sensation of let-down and having been cheated was enormous. It didn't occur to me that anything might be wrong with me until much later. So when I met Jim in Europe and he was nice to me before breakfast, it was a kind of revelation and you can understand why I was so relieved. Just the old chestnut about women having to feel emotional, I suppose. That's what Jim says, anyway. So the losing of my precious virginity was very definitely a non-event.

As to your other question — it has never occurred to me, until recently, that sex was anything other than penetration. Jim certainly behaves as if that is what it is, and having been with him so long and not had any other lovers and not having had to think about it, I just assumed the same. But of course, when I think about it, the real business of penetration is to do with getting pregnant or not — mostly not, I guess.

Years ago, before I joined up with Jim, when I was abroad and very depressed and thinking about chucking it all in and going home, I was getting my only emotional strength from Meg's letters, which were so loving and interesting, and I really wondered if I could make do with her. (Not that I ever put it to her — it was just a question I had to put to myself.) I knew she was gay and I'd reassured her that it made no difference to our friendship, but I couldn't imagine what it was really like to be gay and I wondered if I could settle for her and for our friendship. I never asked her anything about sex between women — I was too shy, I suppose, but it might be because I couldn't imagine it that I decided I couldn't just settle for her — even though she loved me better than anyone had before, and I loved her too — I still do. No one understands me so well — no one else is so sensitive. She has the most refined mind I know. So I can see that thinking of sex as pure penetration must have biased my decision somehow.

I haven't told her any of this — I don't know why I'm telling you — I don't usually open up with people I don't know very well. Maybe you're right — these things are somehow in the air. I don't know. But I still can't see how any of what I'm telling you could be in any way *political*, as you claim. Do keep writing though.

Love,
Frances

ટ✤

Amy to Meg

6 May

Dear Meg,

I don't know why, but I've got such a foreboding about you — sixth sense, all that nonsense. Tried to phone you a couple of times and left messages on your answering machine, but you haven't come back to me. Are you all right? Please reassure me. I get these silly feelings about people sometimes — people who are close to me — and I know it's nonsense but they're strong and I want to be reassured. Perhaps it's because I haven't heard from you since that funny note you sent just before Frances left.

Do write. I'm worried about you.

My love,
Amy

ટ✤

Meg to Amy

7 May

Dear Amy,

Your letter was such an irony but you couldn't know that. I've been paralysed for the last few weeks, unable to say anything, unable to think.

Your 'sixth sense' was right. Jim was here. Frances' husband. He bloody *raped* me. I don't know what to do about it. I can't seem to write about it. It looks so silly, that sentence. He raped me. . . what does that say? Just words.

8 May

Couldn't go on with this letter yesterday. Disoriented. I
shall try and calm down and write it all down exactly as it
happened.

Jim came as expected on the due date, to stay for five days
between Paris and Dublin. It was a Friday and, unusually, Jan
happened to be out that night. Simon was asleep upstairs.

Oh God, I *still* haven't started at the beginning. I've known
Frances for twelve years and loved her intensely almost since
the first meeting — a five-hour lunch in a coffee shop which
went on into supper. We didn't even notice dusk falling, being
in that rare state of rapture with one another's minds. Years
after that, she married Jim, who was more than ten years
older, on the playwright circuit, divorced, openly vulgar and
self-aggrandizing, in a jokey sort of way. She didn't tell
anyone, including me, that they were going to marry. Some of
her friends couldn't cope — others, like myself, thought it our
duty to cope — in fact, to be friendly and non-judgmental.
Anyway, having grown up lesbian in the days before feminism, when lesbianism was a sick and dirty word, I was
convinced that (a) I knew nothing about heterosexual relationships which I assumed were totally and completely different
from lesbian ones and (b) I owed it to society and my friends
to accept marriage as primary and inviolate. So I did my best
towards Jim and everything went all right — he didn't take
any interest in me and Frances and I continued our friendship,
mostly by mail after I came to live here.

Jim had been to stay before, on visits abroad. Imagine, then,
that I had no reason whatever to think he might make a pass
at me — especially since Frances was always going on about
him and how good the marriage was and how much she
missed him and so on.

Anyway, I put the boy to bed and prepared a meal for Jim.
He arrived, as previously, with a bottle of duty-free and a bag
of stinking washing. He'd sat on trains for three weeks in the
same underclothes and waited for our washing machine to do
its magic. I dumped the stuff into buckets to soak, privately

thanking God I didn't have a husband, and got on with the food. As usual, I had a bottle of wine and a candle on the table — nothing out of the ordinary. He'd eaten with us dozens of times, as have most friends. We ate — he boasted about Paris and so on. I don't know why, but I didn't sense anything of what he must have been intending. I went out to make the coffee. It was about nine o'clock.

When I came back he was naked from the waist down. He had an erection. I said 'God, is that supposed to be a sight for sore eyes?' My immediate thought was 'How revolting!' He just grinned, making it clear that this was no joke. I registered that it was for real. I couldn't believe it — I started feeling really frightened.

He leered at me and said we ought to 'have a good hump now.' I felt a rush of things at once, all jumbled, some of them only coming back to me now, as if I'd had an anaesthetic. I know I felt sick, but more than anything, I was terrified. No one was home and the boy was upstairs.

His face was like something out of Hogarth. Grinning, leering, devilish — a beast-man — and the horrifying part was the way he kept on joking, laughing, talking without stopping. I was too terrified to shout. I mouthed things like a fish — open, shut, with nothing coming out. I think I whimpered. I tried to run away but nothing happened — my feet wouldn't move, like a nightmare. All my conditioning rose up in me and choked me. All those times my father took me aside to warn me of the dangers of 'provoking' men. All those 'jokes' about cockteasing. 'Don't tease a man with an erection — he'll go at you like a mad bull' — that sort of thing. I thought if I made a fuss he'd beat hell out of me, beat Simon, smash everything.

He grabbed hold of me, still grinning. Yanked at my clothes. I was begging 'no, no' and 'Don't', but he just laughed. When I said 'what about Frances?' he just laughed even more.

I'd never been forced before and didn't know the extent of my own terror — like thinking you're about to be killed. He pushed me onto the floor. He was still talking — about blue movies, Spanish women, horrendous things — I can't remember it all, not that part. He turned himself end-on to me, pinning my arms down with his knees' — started licking me in a disgusting, horrible, heavy way which hurt like hell — like a leather belt. At the same time he tried to shove his penis into my mouth. His balls were pressing all over my face. I gagged. He said I should suck him off — that that was 'one of the refinements'. I was past choice. I heard my head saying 'placate, placate' but my guts were saying 'even if I get killed, I can't suck him off. Just can't.'

Then he turned round and got nasty — wanted to know what turned me on. 'Nothing, I'm a lesbian,' I sobbed. I was shaking and giggling and crying to stop myself screaming — I knew once I started I'd just scream and scream. 'I'm a lesbian' I hissed, over and over. He said 'Oh yes, I'm very interested in that.'

Then he forced himself into me. It was so painful, I can't tell you — like being stabbed. I was so tight — my body just resisted all by itself — and my cunt was dry as a bone. Apart from the appalling pain between my legs, I was numb all over.

Afterwards he got up and started talking again, as if nothing had happened. I knew I'd been raped and I felt desperate — completely helpless. My intuition told me I mustn't tell Jan. She'd throw him out and that would be the end of my friendship with Frances. *I couldn't bear that thought.* I hope you can understand; whatever the pain and fear and humiliation, my bond with Frances is much more important. Anyway, I knew the police would never believe me in a million years. I'd cooked for the swine — got wine and candles — wasn't cut to pieces. I knew how it would look.

I just had to get through the next few days without saying anything. Had to try to make sure I wasn't left alone with Jim. When Jan came back we were sitting there seeming quite normal, with him going on about Paris.

Saturday was all right. Jan was home all day and he went off to see producers or something. I was in some hinterland of

unreality. He was jokey as usual and Jan was her social self
and already I was wondering if I'd made it up or had a bad
dream or was going mad.

It was like after Simon was born. I'd had a long labour. He
finally came out round about the change in shift time — in
the afternoon — and suddenly from a room full of people,
there was no one. They'd whisked the baby off somewhere
and left me with my legs strapped up, waiting to be stitched.
They said someone would bring a cup of tea. I didn't want any
tea — I wanted my baby, but he wasn't there. I stayed like
that for forty minutes. I could see the clock on the wall. The
doctor didn't come — he said later he'd been really busy.
Well, in the end, I started thinking it hadn't happened. I
hadn't really had a baby. It was all being on the edge of
madness — having some particularly potent dream —
shouting and crying at empty space. No one to hear. Thinking, at the same time, that one shouldn't make a fuss. Then I
thought, if I have had a baby, and they've taken him away,
they might give me some other baby. How will I know he's
mine? I only saw his face for a minute.

Amy, I'm telling you all this so you'll understand why I
kept quiet — how I was able to. I really thought maybe it
hadn't happened. Jan had a call from her mother on Sunday
morning. Her mother was ill and she said she had to rush
over. I could only have stopped her by begging her to stay
with me — which she wouldn't have understood at all, unless
I'd told her why. So she went off and he tried again. Now I
was in a play, rather than a nightmare. At least his need to
force me wasn't so strong. And something in me was
determined not to let him know that I was afraid. Jan took
Simon. The bastard came down for breakfast in his stinking
long-johns and chased me around the kitchen with another
erection sticking out. I coped better this time. The sun was
shining and I wasn't so shocked. I just kept saying no no no
no no — whatever chat he went on with — and in the end I
said why didn't he go back upstairs and relieve himself if he
was as desperate as that, and he laughed and said oh no, that

would be a waste. I said no over and over and then he got
bored and asked if I had a Sunday paper. The erection was still
there and I wished more than anything that I didn't have to
look at it. He grabbed me round the waist and said again
'Come on, humping before breakfast, that's what I like. That's
a good idea.' I went on resisting and after about half an hour
he disappeared upstairs. Then Jan came back. For the rest of
the time I wasn't alone with him and I made sure Jan wasn't
either. But I didn't tell anyone.

On the last day, Jan popped out for a specified half hour,
just next door, and he started telling more of his funny stories
about himself and I blurted out at him that I couldn't see
what he was up to, considering Frances was his wife and so
fond of him and I was her friend. 'Oh', he said, 'fornicating
with Frances' friends is one of my things. But you don't tell. I
believe in good taste. You don't tell. That would be in bad
taste.' He has that sort of style — laying down the laws of
God as if he had invented them. The sort of vulgarity that
goes with never questioning one's own judgments.

I had thought at the time that the whole thing was so night-
marish — so unreal — that it couldn't possibly have anything
to do with me at all. That it was his way of making sure that
Frances and I could not go on being so close. So when he said
he 'fornicated' with all her friends I began to see that it was a
power trip for him, where he could get rid of any opposing
source of human feeling she might have other than him, by
suborning it. I wondered what all these other friends had done
about it. Jim obviously never 'told' and I suppose they didn't
either.

He talked and talked. It is all imprinted on my brain as if by
some form of torture. He elaborated on this — I had a pain in
my chest because of Frances. He said 'I don't smoke cigarettes
and I don't stuff other women. I say that. That's a thing about
me. But Frances knows I smoke at rehearsals. And when I'm
away, I don't see why I should live like a monk. I'm attractive. Women want me and I say so if I want them. It
happened a couple of times just this last week. Once was on a

train. I've got beautiful hands, for example.' It's so ironic, Amy. Frances had said to me when she was here that she didn't like Jim smoking at rehearsals and pretending he hadn't. She said she couldn't explain it and that she must be neurotic about it but that it felt as if he had taken a mistress! God. . . . (Have to go. The boy's home from playschool. This letter is turning into a book. . . .)

9 May

It's helping to write all this down. I've been so depressed. It's my friendship with Frances that's uppermost in my mind — how not to lose it. I asked Jim whether he thought Frances 'lived like a monk' when he was away. I remember him sitting back, lighting a cigarette and saying 'She doesn't ever want anyone else. I satisfy her.'

He didn't mean, he assured me, that he thought she never got an offer. He said men like Frances because she's 'asexual'. Imagine! He added that she dresses well and that he liked that. 'When she goes anywhere with me, men like her. And I like that,' he said. My friend Frances, whom I've loved and admired, was being spoken of as some little woman who did what she was told and needed only Jim for all her human needs.

Now that I write this I get clearer about my instinct that he couldn't cope with her having anyone important outside him. I can't forget a word the bastard said. It went on: 'She'll come back to Paris with me. She can have that out with the administration when she gets back to work. They'll have to understand that she's not just the Department — she's married to a famous playwright and if I've got to go away for two or three months then she's got to come with me and they'll have to understand that. If they want to keep her they'll have to understand that. I'll come to London for three months later on to put my play on. But there's no way Frances will come for three months. We don't like London *that* much. She might come for three weeks. If she's not going to coach for me, she doesn't need to be in London for longer than three weeks. She

likes San Francisco. Her couple of friends are in San
Francisco. So if she goes anywhere for three months, it'll be
San Francisco. But she'll go to Paris for three months with
me. Oh yes, she'll do that. I think I've handled it all very well.
Very well. She got the job and I didn't make a fuss about it. I
let her do it. I think she's entitled to that. But I think I
handled it very well. She can do that for another ten or
twenty years. Then she can do her big piece. She ought to do
one big piece, I think. Because she's got talent. She'll be all
right. I think when I get back I'll get her to write another little
piece about me. Oh, I think she should do that. If you look at
my press-cuttings, you'll see she did a lot of little pieces about
me. But the last one was a couple of years ago. I think it's time
she did another one. I think she should do another one when I
get back.'

I can hear him saying all this as clearly as if it were still
happening. I suppose I couldn't believe it, that my sensitive,
diffident, loving Frances lived in the same universe and was
being described in this awful way by such a pig. Oh, then he
said he didn't miss her the way she missed him when they
were separated. He said 'That's one thing I hope Women's Lib
won't change. I think women ought to be half the number of
doctors and professors and politicians. I believe in that. But I
don't want their irrationality to change. I don't want to read
all that Masters and Johnson. I'd rather see it all at the
movies. Women in the movies, that's what I like! By which
he meant blue movies, which Frances had once told me he
went to with some male crony, and which disturbed her, for
some reason, but she wasn't sure why.

It's helping me to write all this down. I've been so
disoriented. When I've been alone — in the bath or somewhere
— I've suddenly burst out crying. I feel such fury and helpless-
ness. My relationship with Jan is in a mess, because I didn't
tell her the truth and I've never hidden anything important
before. Dialogues go on in my head. I can't work properly —
my concentration has gone to pieces. I can't find anything
which I've done wrong but I feel so punished. I get depressed

when I think Frances won't be able to cope with all this.
When I look at Simon I'm happy I'm not pregnant. Jan keeps
saying what's the matter, asking why I'm so withdrawn. I
can't explain it to her. I'm just paralysed somehow. I'm
frightened about working it out with Frances though I know
I'll have to. I think if I ever see that pig again I'll vomit.

It's helped me a lot to get all this written down, but I still
don't know what to do about it. I can't seem to write to
Frances at all and I must. We've always written. She'll know
something is wrong — well, *you* knew something was wrong
— and I don't know either how to tell her or how to not tell
her.

No more now. My love,
Meg

ই♥

Amy to Meg

11 May

My dear Meg,

I've just this minute finished reading your letter. Oh dearest
Meg!

But God and Christ! Whatever is the matter with you? How
could you let this bastard get away with treating you (and
Frances) like that? Yes, I'm angry and I shouldn't be, and even
while I'm writing this I know I don't mean to vent my anger
on you — that's what women have been conditioned to do, to
divert it from the culprits, who are the men. Frances and I
have been writing to each other since she went back and her
letters have been so positive — about you, about herself,
about the new ideas she's thinking about, and also about her
marriage and how much she cares about 'her Jim'. Is it really
such an insane world we live in? I knew he was an ordinary
egotist, as all men are who haven't been feminised in one way
or another, but there's a difference between the ordinary
egotist and the pig.

You *have* to tell Frances, of course you must. Her love for
you is very strong, and anyway truth is always easier to deal

with than evasion. And it sounds as if it has happened before, so she can't, surely, not know. The fact that she's never let on about it is not unusual — many women don't.

He's obviously gone now. But Meg, what about Jan? She must know too. *Don't let him get away with it.* I can't write any more now. I'll try tomorrow. I might think of something.

Love,
Amy

12 May

I've let my letter of yesterday stand, although I'm ashamed of it now that I'm calm again. It was my honest reaction and it teaches me a lot about what *I* still have to learn in this matter. I turned on you, as if you had willfully or willingly betrayed yourself. What really happened was that you were overpowered by the oppressor — not surprising. He came in the guise of a friend — the wolf in sheep's clothing. You're right — the police would never do anything. You wouldn't have a case at all. They would say he didn't even beat you up. I realised, in the depths of my unconsciousness last night, that inside myself is the same myth that all women are taught to collude in. You're the first woman who I've been really close to who has had this experience. The myth is that somehow the woman has asked for it. She hasn't been careful enough. She has let out unconscious seductive signals. And the poor man has this strong, natural sex drive that he some-how can't control. . . God, let me humble myself to you as much as I decently can. I'm sorry, really.

We have to think rationally what you should do. I'm sure you agree that Frances must be told. You owe it to her as her friend. It's always the wife who is the last to be told — so much for our sisterhood if we perpetuate that. But what ramifications that will have, I can't say. Oh Meg, let me know how I can help you, if at all. My love goes out to you,

Amy

Meg to Amy

15 May

Dear friend Amy,

Thank you for being so honest and frank with me. I was
of course hurt when I began to read your letter, but then I
understood your own explanation of your initial reaction and
the echo bells went in my mind.

And then I started wondering whether it was somehow my
fault for providing the wine and food, or for being alone, or for
not fighting and kicking and biting and screaming, or for not
having the sort of magical presence which is assumed to keep
men at bay. My fault. When I ought to be able to be sure it
was *his* fault. He has committed a *crime*, I keep telling
myself, but the words are empty and I don't know how to get
straight with Frances. I sat down to write to her and wrote to
you instead. Underneath, I have this growing contempt for
her, which I can't handle, have never had before (quite the
opposite!) and I want to nip it in the bud and feel equal with
her again. But how can I feel equal when she's living with
such a pig? What can I say?

I've been talking to Clare, a friend who was at university
with Frances years ago. She was very sympathetic, having
previously (but silently, to herself) banned Jim from her flat.
She said she asked them both to dinner after they were
married (that mistake we all make!) and he just marched in
and said 'Where's the food?', took a plate and plonked himself
in front of the television for the evening. Clare found it so
insulting she told me she decided never to invite him again.
But she didn't say that to Frances. How can one? Anyway,
Clare said to me that Frances would never believe it in a
million years and that if I told her, I would lose the
friendship. I'd be forcing her to choose between me and her
marriage and she'd have to choose her marriage. She (Clare)
was very definite about this, and she's a shrewd judge of
people, so I feel more depressed than ever. How can I go on
with the friendship if I have a secret like this, when we've
never kept anything from each other and when it makes me

feel contempt that I have to protect such an awful man and such an awful marriage? But why should I be forced, on the other hand, to give up a friendship that has meant so much to me? More than any other, in fact? I don't know what to do.

You asked if you could help. Please keep writing to Frances as you were before, without mentioning any of this of course. Perhaps you could hint that I've been exceptionally busy and rather unwell and will write as soon as I can.

Until next time. In sisterhood,

Meg

ॐ

Amy to Frances

17 May

Dear Frances,

Thanks for your letter, which I'm not sure how to answer. I want to be really honest with you and yet feel constrained by the usual socialised politeness one has been trained to. In a less dangerous world I might just go on saying to you that I can understand, that we're all different, that everyone's perception somehow has equal validity, even though our perceptions are contradictory and juxtaposed, and so on. Can I dare to be honest with you? Are women's bonds so fragile that I even need to ask?

I want to ask you whether what you say about Jim and your relationship with him is really the truth. Whether you're sure it isn't a picture of how you would like it to be, rather than how it really is. You will wonder why I should question you like this. I can't and won't go into that now, except to say that I'm not clear about why you accept what seems to be a totally submissive position in your marriage when in all other areas of your life, especially your work, you are so independent and confident.

And you haven't said anything about the reaction your friends and family and so on have had towards Jim. That's important too, isn't it? What does Meg think of him, for example? What would you do if you found that Jim had some-

how caused pain to Meg? Would that be a situation of divided
loyalties or would you blindly accept that whatever Jim said
or did would be something you would be automatically
expected to support and accept?

In my own case, you see, I have slowly learned to put my
relationship with Tim on the line — learned to respond positively to the feelings and reactions of my women friends, so
that I can give to women what is their right. I resist the idea
that Tim should have automatic ascendancy. How that works
in practice is that he makes the space and time for me to meet
regularly with my women friends or to do whatever other
women's work I'm involved in, takes over the child-minding
or housework if an important women's issue comes up which
has priority, and so on. We agree that politically women's
issues have priority because women under a patriarchal
system are the oppressed group, and that even though Tim
wishes to repudiate his white male supremacy, because it is a
'class privilege', he still enjoys the benefits of his superiority,
whether he wants to or not — like being able to walk alone at
night without fear of rape. He chooses positively to support
the ending of patriarchy and its institutionalisation of male
privilege and that is why in ordinary daily living he supports
the prior claims of women's work.

It takes a fair amount of consciousness-raising and commitment for a man to reach that position — we've had to spend
years at it. But it's worth it, Frances. Don't fall for the mirage
of having a relationship under any circumstances just because
you don't want to face being lonely. If the terms aren't
straightforward between you, you'll get hurt in the end anyway — badly hurt.

Tim and I had a holiday together recently — just the two of
us. It was such a blissful time and I thought how all the work
and struggle was really worth it. The relief of having a relationship where one can be equal and trusting is better than
anything I ever had before. My marriage, by contrast, had
been merely a series of contretemps, frustrations and repres-
sions, because only I was motivated to change and grow —

my ex-husband never knew what I was talking about. Moving out and meeting Tim was the best thing I ever did for myself. Do think about some of this. Have you heard from Meg?

Love,
Amy

ॐ

Frances to Amy

20 May

Dear Amy,
   A piece of graffiti in our ladies' lavatory — thought it might amuse you —

PENETRATION

is

invasion   evasion   manipulation   capitulation

   It amused me — and then I wondered why I was laughing. I don't really understand such an idea. Anyway, how can you have sex without penetration? I know about stimulation and so on — but it doesn't feel like real sex, does it? I know Germaine Greer wrote that somewhere — that she'd rather make love with a full cunt than an empty one. And it's in the Hite Report too. Maybe I laughed because it's all so extreme and absurd to me, whatever you say. I don't mean to hurt your feelings when you've been so open about your relationship with Tim, but it just isn't for me, I'm sure.
   I can't answer your questions about Jim. I believe in loyalty. If any of my friends said anything against him, whatever I thought about it, I would stick by him and the friend or friends would have to go. Even Meg. I told you I thought about that years ago and decided I couldn't get by with just Meg, so if it came to a choice, it would have to be Jim, much as my heart would hurt like hell underneath. I can't see how my life could be based on my female friendships, unless I were gay, which I'm not.

Still, I love Meg as intensely as I can. I can't understand
why she hasn't written. I've only had a short note since I got
back. Is she all right? However busy she is, she usually finds
time to write to me, especially when we've met again after a
longish period. She's so unnerving sometimes — one minute
all passion and endless time and interest — the next, nothing
and silence. I wonder if you're suggesting there was some sort
of argument with Jim while he was staying with her? If there
was, she should know better than to worry about it. I'm not
such a stupid cow that I would attack her for that. Now I'm
fantasising. . . what was behind your questions? You talk
about being honest and so on, but I'm not clear about what
your letter and questions mean. Has something happened that
I don't know about?

I wish I could join you, sympathise, understand. I just don't
feel constantly oppressed. I get tired of Jim being so
demanding and asking me to write articles about him and do
all his typing when I'm trying to get on with my own work —
but he's such a child in most respects that I think that's just
another aspect of the same thing.

For example, I shop and cook and make good vegetarian
food for us, which he says he likes and which I know he feels
better on than all the greasy muck he used to eat, but I know
when I'm not around, he goes to the nearest hamburger joint
and stuffs himself on junk food. I feel a bit hurt about it, and I
think it's silly, but what is the point of getting in a twit about
it? I can't change it, and anyway, as I said, it's a childlike
characteristic. And everyone, including my mum, always says
that men are like children. Just humour them and they'll be
nice to you. What's wrong with it? I don't feel harmed by it
and anyway I don't want to spend my life alone. I get
depressed easily enough, and Jim is so dynamic and life with
him is so busy that the time gets filled up without my
noticing and I don't get so depressed.

I don't want continual confrontation with reality —
couldn't handle it. Don't you know that line of Eliot's —
'Humankind cannot bear very much reality' — very true, at

least for me. Sometimes, secretly, I hanker after what you're
describing — but I know I can't have it.

                                        Love,
                                        Frances

                        ટે✦

Frances to Meg

                                        20 May

Dear Meg,
   Are you all right? I can't understand why you haven't
written. We had such a happy time together and now no
word. Have I offended you in some way? I'm not aware, if I
have, but if I have, I'm sorry and wish you would tell me.
Nothing is more ambiguous than silence. Or has something
happened? If so, tell me about it. You're so important to me
and I can't bear the idea that you would keep back any
problems. Whatever it might be, we can handle it as we've
always handled everything before. I care about you — you
know that.
   My work is going fine since I got back. I had such a real
shot in the arm from my time with you — and, I must admit,
from not having to cope with you-know-who's advances,
having made sure I was not alone with him, except in public
places — that I've begun the article I was blocking on before I
came away. Jim came back last week — that has also made
me feel considerably better — I'm such a poor fish alone and I
like having him around — in fact, I need to have him around.
He also seems to have had a good time and is busy with some
new project to do with one of the theatre-cafés in town. I
don't specially like him being out so late three nights a week,
but then. . . . It's nice to be home. Foreign climes are okay
but I often feel once I've tramped over one lot of old stones
then the next dozen lots of stones are much the same. I'm no
adventurer.
   It's a bit annoying that although I've got the drive now to
get on with my paper, Jim is at me all the time to do another
little 'piece' on him, as he calls my reviews of his work, for

the *Echo*. The whole thing embarrasses me. I don't really think it's okay to go on and on extolling him in public as if we didn't know each other — and anyway I want some space for myself before another 'low' turns up and I can't get on again. But he thinks his getting famous and staying that way is really important to both of us and that since I've got a job, that should be enough for me — which I suppose it is, most of the time. Oh dear, he's so demanding somehow.

I thought about our conversation about babies all the way back, and on and off since being home again, but back on my own patch I see how impossible it would be to discuss. I have to stick to what we've agreed. You know Jim's conditions for our marriage — no wedding, no children and no being financially supported. How can I break the agreement now? It's against my sense of honour, even though seeing you with Simon made the whole thing much more real and very painful. You can't have everything, Meg — and it's necessary to settle for what there is. I admire your ability always to ask for more, but I'm not as strong as you are. In fact, very few people are so strong. They mostly learn to accept what there is and to be content with it.

I suppose you could never live with someone like Jim — you're pretty demanding yourself — but that's what I've chosen and that's what I must stick to. And I still have my nice little fantasy life with my books, and I have my little house and my little cat — I can manage with little things. I know you will think I'm craven and wasting myself, as you always say when we're talking about books and writing, and you are a great source of strength to me, but you know all that about leopards and spots. . . . I can't turn into a big person overnight, if at all. Please don't despise me — your respect and encouragement is always so vital and keeps me going more than you know.

I think I've always loved you.

Frances

Meg to Frances

26 May

Dear Frances,

Thanks for your letter. I'm sorry to have been out of touch. I haven't been specially well and I've also been unusually busy. I know this is only a card and we both feel disappointed to get only a card but I can't manage any more just at the moment. I'll write when I can.

My love as always,
Meg

ॐ

Amy to Meg

26 May

Dear Meg,

Thanks for your letter. I feel for you. If your friend Clare is right then it's not much of a choice. And if she is right that is something Jim would have known all the time. He would be the winner by having humiliated you, humiliated Frances in your eyes (and in his own, which might also be something he needs to do) and managed to destroy the friendship which he must, for all his boasting and seeming self-confidence, have found extremely threatening. If it takes a violent act to destroy something, then the strength of the something was powerful enough to be reckoned with. Not that that's much comfort.

But Clare might be wrong. Frances may be more resilient than she thinks, when faced with a *real* situation. You know her, it seems, better than anyone, so you will have to judge about that. But whatever the risk, I still don't see how you can not tell her. You would begin to despise her and that would poison the trust in your friendship and you would therefore lose her anyway. Don't you think? She doesn't seem to me to be such a frightened little mouse and, as you have always said, she's got a brain as hard as steel. And she said, anyway, that Jim had been fooling around with her best friend before she married him. I can't think she'd be so deliberately blind and masochistic to be a hundred per cent shocked. Don't you, in the end, have to trust *her* strength and resources, as well as the bond of your friendship? I wish I could come and talk it over with you but it's just impossible at the moment. Tell me what you decide, anyway.

Love and thoughts,
Amy

ह◆

Meg to Frances

5 June

Dear Frances,

I promised I'd write and I didn't. Forgive me. Something has come up. Among other things, I find I have to read some manuscripts housed at Yale and have got some travel money for three weeks. I'll therefore be in the States at the beginning of next month and wonder if I can come and see you on the weekend of the 14th. I can't stay — there isn't time — I have another person to see about the book on the 16th in New York. Of course, if you wanted to come down to meet me, that would be even better — wonderful, in fact. But I don't know what your schedule is like. Let me know, anyway.

Love,
Meg

ह◆

Frances to Meg

16 June

Dear Meg,

How super! An unexpected trip. You sound so mysterious these days. I stopped worrying about you, thinking that if something bad had happened I'd have known about it by now, although I admit I've been hurt by your not writing properly, so to speak. You can tell me about it, though, in the flesh. No, I can't make it to New Haven or New York — that's the weekend when the Department has its annual non-student party — visiting academics being shown the ropes and so on. But the 14th I shall certainly devote to you, at least the afternoon of it. Let's meet at the old cafe if you like. Two o'clock. Or if you want me to come to the airport, let me know about your flight and so on. If I don't hear, I'll expect you at two in the cafe. Can hardly wait. I'll show you my article which I'll have finished by then, with any luck, and if Jim stops nagging me about doing his 'piece', as he keeps calling it. Men, honestly!

See you soon,

Love,
Frances

8❧

Amy to Meg

18 June

Dear Meg,

What's happened? I haven't had a reply to my last letter. Did I upset you? Are you too depressed to write? It must be three weeks since I've heard. Do drop me a card at least.

In sisterhood. *And* solidarity,

Amy

8❧

Frances to Amy

18 June

Dear Amy,

I'm so elated! As I expect you know, Meg is coming over here for three weeks — she has to do some work at Yale and we're arranging to see each other at least over one of the weekends. It's not the best time for me — lots of things going on in the Department — but it's so good to have something like that come out of the blue. I think Meg must have been very busy as well as she hasn't written since I was with you all, apart from a couple of cards.

Jim is driving me mad at present about his 'piece' and about another load of typing. I wish he could get someone else to do it. He could afford a secretary but it seems to be important that I do it — and I suppose, deep down, I like feeling useful and needed. I just wish it wasn't so much, or so often. That would be one plus, living with Meg instead of Jim — at least she would do her own typing! What do you think? Do you think lesbians have an easier time of it? Easier lifestyle? Meg always seems to get everything done that she intends to — and even since she's had her baby, she's still been able to carry on all her other work and activities. But even if they do have an easier time, it's no use to me — if I'm not one of them, I can't join in. You have to be born a lesbian, don't you? I mean, I can't imagine having my sex life with another woman — I don't seem to have any of the requisite feelings. Have you ever tried it? I'm too shy to discuss it with Meg. We always avoided talking about it too much — it was somehow embarrassing, for her as much as for me. Except that she used to say that if one loved somebody, it would be impossible to hate that person's body, which I think is true. What do you think?

Love and best wishes,
Frances

ह∾

Amy to Frances

23 June

Dear Frances,

Thanks for your letter. Hope you and Meg have a good time together when you meet. To answer some of your questions: no, I don't think women are born lesbian. Those who are lesbian have more independence and courage than the rest of us, having broken through the weight of conditioning, social approval, expectation, feminine image, and so on. They are the women I most often admire, because they really are doing it by themselves. In a patriarchal system, women who stand with other women in defiance of male supremacy, and who

are demanding freedom and equality, are showing the
healthiest possible response to the unhealthy situation we
were all born into. Masters and Johnson even say that unless
men adjust very promptly to the now-clear evidence about
women's sexuality, it will become a natural response for more
and more women to become lesbian. As for my own case, I
was one of the more cowed ones who became conventionally
conditioned, got married, had a child, kept house, and so on.
Becoming a feminist gave me the strength to leave my
marriage and to begin my relationship with Tim.

Lesbianism has not, up till now, anyway, been an
emotional alternative for me. Something about the close
identification possible between two women is a threat to my
hard-won autonomy. My sense of myself is too precious to
me to face the prospect of perhaps having to give part of it
away. To me, a woman is an equal, and my sister, and I
would therefore find it much more difficult to deny her, or to
confront her, than I do a man, from whom I can legitimately
claim priority for my need to rebuild the positive self that
traditional femininity — put on us by men — has crippled. A
lesbian relationship takes place on common ground, between
equals — a heterosexual relationship, under patriarchy, is not
between equals. I strive, with and against Tim, all the time to
achieve that equality, but the whole weight of the culture is
against the struggle.

This is not to say I am heterosexual purely out of fear —
that I am only with Tim because I am afraid of being with a
woman. We have struggled so much together that our basic
and real liking for one another has developed into a deep
trust. Seeing how he has changed — how he still changes — is
a source of excitement and optimism for me, as well as being
a reason to go on believing in creativity and love. He evokes
my most tender feelings — well, not all the time, of course —
but basically. Together — and separately — we are finding a
more enduring bond than the caprice of passion. I don't have a
special sensual response to him just because he is a man.
Consciousness-raising brings one beyond that. Indeed, one of

the things all women can become aware of is their own lesbian potential. It isn't as far below the surface as all that. If lesbianism were really a small minority behaviour — and if it were really well repressed — the patriarchy would not be so threatened by it. Scores of previously married women are happily forming lesbian relationships without turning a hair.

Which brings me to something else. As a *political* alternative — a behaviour and lifestyle consistent with feminist aims — lesbianism has become a major strategy. I *personally* — and I stress the 'personally' — am not able to take this step, regardless of my commitment to Tim. I can't and won't go to bed with a woman just out of political principle — mine or anyone else's. Apart from the idea being alien to my sense of autonomy, I think the heterosexual revolution is worth fighting as well. That is my battleground. Nevertheless I stand with the lesbian sisters and I support them utterly.

As to your other questions: no, they most certainly do not have an easier life-style. They do not enjoy any protection from social institutions. Think how protected you and I can be just because we have a marriage certificate and a wedding ring. These devices immediately divide the female population — which is what they are meant to do. It would not suit patriarchy for all women to feel solidarity together. Lesbian women know this, and fight it in very many different ways, but mostly by the way they live. Many of them might not admit to that, might even say they are 'not political' and are only living their private lives like anyone else — but whether it is clear to them or not, it is very clear to me. They live independently from male privilege — they do not succour men, nor do they need them. In other words, lesbians are the only women who can be seen to treat men as their equals and to assume with men that they, the women, are equal. That is what I think screws up the men when they meet lesbians — either they are very sexually turned on because they see a challenge to their masculinity ('all they need is a good fuck, which I can give them') — or they are enraged by the possibility that their masculinity is being rejected ('filthy

creatures — unnatural, unclean' etc). As far as Meg is
concerned, you have known her much longer and better than I
have, so you must know the answer to your own question. I
can't see how anyone could say she has an easy life. An open
lesbian has always to defend her position and cannot look
forward to any respite from that defensive stance. Only other
lesbians will give any support, and, latterly, some heterosexual feminists as well.

I feel, if I may say so, that you shy away from all this and
somehow you think you can leave the lesbian issue out of
your friendship with Meg — but I venture to suggest that you
won't be able to go on doing that for ever. I don't mean I think
it's all you — Meg has colluded in the evasion — but the state
of feminism, quite apart from the dynamics between the two
of you, will mean that you will both have to get your feelings
much more out into the open. The lesbian alternative is
something that *all* women, in the end, will have to consider
consciously. No doubt it will take another century in some
parts of the world — but in our culture it's a matter of years
only.

It's the same kind of consciousness growth as we've seen
with racism; in some cultures it is still possible to think of
'superior' and 'inferior' races, whereas to others it has been
becoming obvious that such a stance is impossible — morally,
economically and 'scientifically' just not possible. Sooner or
later the white South Africans will have to accept their black
citizens' partnership, or seek asylum elsewhere. But wherever
they go, they will find the concept of slavery impossible and
will have to adjust. In the same way, male superiority is
historically doomed — and the connection between patriarchy
and the hostility shown towards lesbianism will become
obvious with hindsight. The historians of the future will find
our attitudes as hard to comprehend as we find the witch-
hunts of the sixteenth and seventeenth centuries. We forget
that they took place a mere three centuries ago. We forget
that within the last five hundred years the Church was
still arguing about whether or not women had souls. We

forget that it is only in our own century that we have been
allowed to vote; that we have been officially allowed to ask
for an abortion; that we have been officially allowed to ask for
contraception; that we have achieved a nominal equality in
the divorce courts; and so on.

We have yet to accept, as a society, that a woman has the
right to choose her mode of sexual conduct, and that having
done so, she is entitled to the same respect for her privacy as
her sisters. Any suggestion of showing 'pity', 'charity' or other
'compassionate' attitudes towards lesbian women ought to be
rigorously challenged and rooted out. Meg should not be
having a harder life than the rest of us just because she has
chosen to live independently from men and to live in positive
partnership with women. Don't you see how the unconscious
attitude of superiority which the rest of us have been taught
to hold actually in the end poisons friendships by subverting
the parity that friends share? It is something that cannot
finally be avoided, however attractive it might be to try in
terms of companionship and lack of confrontation. Please,
Frances, you do see what I mean, don't you?

I look forward to hearing from you soon. Meanwhile love
and solidarity —

Amy

౭✿

Jane to Meg

23 June

Dear Meg,

My trouble, or one of my troubles, is that I'm not a bottom-
less fount of lovingkindness, carping though that may sound
to you. I heard from Amy that you've been ill — but were you
really ill for two whole months? You wrote to me last on 11
April. I must be a fool, in relation to you, don't you think?
Why am I bothering now?

I *resent* having to write my anger to you and resent even
more feeling it, since I want as much as possible to feel

positive things towards the women I care about. But I resent, equally, having my efforts or energy or giving of myself to be taken for granted as if my needs or feelings were of no importance to you. Why should I have to ask Amy how you are?

Now I suppose you will turn hard-hearted on me and tell me I have no right to expect anything from you. Perfectly true. But I do, nevertheless. If I didn't write to you until the middle of August, now, you'd mind, wouldn't you? Perhaps you wouldn't . . . . Do you really *want* to be my friend, when I'm such a purist? If you do, you have to put some effort in.

> Exasperated sisterly
> greetings,
> Jane

ह•

Meg to Jane

27 June

Dear Jane,

I've had your letter. Sorry you feel so strongly. Yes, I think you have no right, but so what? You think you have.

Some bad things have happened to me which have paralysed my mind and life, more or less. I can't write it all down here. You can ask Amy if you want to know. I'll tell her I don't mind if she tells you. I wrote to her because she's met one of the people involved, and if that hurts your feelings, it's too bad. I can't write my life down to everyone or I'd never live any of it. I'm angry with you for being unreasonably (I think) angry with me.

I'm off to America for three weeks next month to do some research on some papers over there — back on 25 July. I'd like you to come and see me. I want to meet you. It's weird having all these disembodied emotions on paper. I want to see what you look like and what sort of voice you have and all that sort of thing. Especially if you take the liberty of

haranguing me by post. I'm sorry if I offended you but for
Christ's sake stop putting pressure on me. You have no right.
I give you no such right. But I want to meet you.

In sisterhood,
Meg

સ◆

Meg to Amy

28 June

Dear Amy,
   Sorry. Thanks for your concern. I've decided I can't handle
this thing with Frances by mail. I'm going to go and see her.
Fly out next week. Got some research money to look at the
papers at Yale which I would have had to do some time so it's
a good excuse. Jane has sent me an angry 'what's-the-silence-
about?' letter. I told her she could ask you. Tell her what she
wants to know. I can't write it all out again. Her ripping into
me like that has pushed me off balance. It shouldn't, but it
has. I shouldn't let it, but I have. What is it about her? Who
the fuck does she think she is? Have we got to put up with
that sort of invasion for the sake of solidarity? Oh God, there's
something about her letters, nevertheless, that makes me like
her. Please explain when she asks.
   I'll write to you after I've seen Frances and tell you what
happened. You're right that I have to tell her, but at least face
to face I'll see the real reaction, which is not necessarily to be
expected from a letter. Anyway, I've written dozens of letters
and thrown them all away. I can't put it to her like that. I
know she hates confrontation, but she knows me, too, and
she knows I've never told her any lies. Why should I?
   Thanks for your concern and support. It's meant a lot to
me.

Love and sisterhood,
Meg

સ◆

Amy to Meg

1 July

Dear Meg,

Thanks for your letter. Don't know if this will reach you before you go, but if it does, good luck. I'll be thinking of you and wishing you and Frances well. I like her.

Jane came to see me this morning. She was rather sheepish at first, saying she wrote you in one of her fits of temper and wished afterwards that she hadn't posted the letter. I think she knows she's got to start doing something about her lack of control — it upsets other people so often. But she was genuinely worried about you, and genuinely hurt that she thought you'd dropped out of communication with her without giving a reason. But when I told her about what Jim had done to you and what sort of conflict you were in about it she flew into such a rage she was almost shaking. I had to stop her picking up the phone and giving Jim's name to the police. I only succeeded by shouting at her about what would happen to you if you were had up for slander. Then she started crying. 'These shit pricks, this shit patriarchy,' she kept saying. Anyway, she calmed down a bit in the end, but I'm telling you all this in case she's at the airport to meet you when you get back — or on your doorstep or something like that. She's determined to see you as soon as possible.

I wish I could come myself, but it's just impossible. I have a strong need to *see* you, which I have to keep suppressing. Some of it, I know, is that I just want to hold you and comfort you, since I'm aware how cold it is to get words on a page and not to have the reassurance of a physical presence. All I can do is to repeat that your friendship is important to me and that the words are not coming from a cold place at all. In a sense, all of us have been raped at least once, but we're mostly not aware of it — and the emotional rape that goes on all the time is not acknowledged as such at all. You've had a particularly blatant and brutalising experience of it, which is why I want to comfort you. But you do see, don't you, that it's only an extreme version of what you had experienced already? Take succour from Jane, anyway. She wants to give it.

Must go. Good luck and safe travelling.

Amy

Frances to Amy

13 July

Dear Amy,

Thanks for your letter. Want to write back before I see Meg tomorrow – in a rush so forgive me if my thoughts are not very ordered. Jim was a bit taken aback when I said Meg was coming but that's natural enough when we all met so recently, I suppose. I feel a bit strange myself, I must admit, having had such brief cards from Meg herself and having had such an intimate correspondence with you, partly about her. I can't answer you properly about the things you say, especially about lesbianism. But there's something I want to tell you. I don't know if Meg has told you already or not. If she has, then you're very discreet. If she hasn't, then she's very discreet. And I, who have always thought I was the epitome of discretion, now see myself writing these words and feel particularly detached.

You see, I've thought for a long time about some of the things you talk about, though not in the same way. I've thought, for example, about the closeness I've always felt with Meg, and how important it has been for me – more important than I wanted to admit to myself and certainly more important than I've conveyed to her, directly, anyway. I can't bear the idea of being a lesbian – or other people thinking I am one – and I can't bear the idea of living alone or losing my marriage, which is somehow an obscure threat in all this, though Meg has never breathed the slightest word about such a possibility. Anyway, I thought how increasingly artificial it was, meeting and having such intimate exchange and always stopping short of any sexual expression of our feeling for each other. So I took a deep breath and asked her

whether she wanted to spend the night with me. And that's
what we did — on my last night there. It was right — I felt
good and warm, but I must admit it was somehow peculiar
not having a penis — that's what I'm used to, after all.
Emotionally it was great. So you can see why I feel strange
about her only writing a couple of cards.

I haven't told Jim yet. I will in the end, but not yet.
Anyway, I'll write again after seeing Meg.

Love,
Frances

ह♥

Meg to Amy

17 July

My dear Amy,

I've got a typewriter room in the library and so won't be
disturbed for hours till they shut the place and all I want to do
is tell you how awful, awful, awful it was. My God. I saw
Frances on the 14th, as arranged. We met in the café where
we used to talk for hours on end. The same instant recognition. The same indescribable and intense warmth. I call it
love because I don't know what else to call it. It's the purest
feeling I've ever had in my life. I've always had it with her.
I always told myself — we always told each other — that it
was nothing to do with sexuality. I know now that that
wasn't true. We must have been in love with each other all the
time, and the passion was somehow fuelled by its non-
consummation, just like in the old Romances. But now it's
dead. After consummation comes death. That's Romantic as
well, isn't it? And now I'm a jumble of emotions, all
disordered — I'm an unholy and unlikely blend of bitterness,
hatred, regret, humiliation, revenge, disillusionment,
unbelief, depression and hurt. The chain is broken. Whatever
happens after this, I can never again have the respect for
Frances which generated how I felt about her. And I suspect
that not being able to feel for her as I have, that I shan't be
able to feel like that with anyone. Is that what it means to

grow up? To be mature? To lose faith and live grey days in a grey world? God, if that's the truth, I hate it. Am filled with loathing for any endeavour. Especially if the chain between women is so weak that a bad man, a really *bad* man, can break it so effortlessly.

Oh Amy, what is the point in feminism if women themselves are so vulnerable, even with each other? Must we be as mad as Jane is to get anywhere? To have a sense of getting anywhere?

But I'm not telling you in the right order. My ego is cracking. I feel so desolate. I can't even write to Jan, apart from the conventional postcard. She knows something's up, but she also knows I can't talk to her about it yet. She senses it's something to do with Frances, but she's always accepted that that's some mysterious closed circle which is nothing to do with her. I feel as bad as I did when I lost my first pregnancy. Grief, with no way of covering the rawness of the wound.

Oh God, start again. I saw her in the café and we chatted about this and that and she showed me her latest article and we discussed that. Then she produced her bit about Jim for the *Echo* which she wanted me to read. She was so pleased with herself for having got them both finished in time to be able to show me and ask my opinion. I couldn't handle it any longer. I knew then, whatever Clare said, that your instinct, and mine, were the right ones and that I had to come out with it, whatever the consequences. I said I couldn't read the article just then but that there was a problem about Jim that I had to talk to her about. I started to cry. She got up and came around to my side of the table and put her arms around me and said, 'Sweetheart, whatever is the matter?' The 'sweetheart' undid me even more. That's to do with something I haven't told *anybody* till now. When she was staying with me, on the last night, when Jan was away with Simon for the weekend, and we had been having one of our long talks, very late, I said in the end 'I suppose we'd better go to bed now'. And she looked at me strangely and said 'Would you like me to stay?' For a minute or two I didn't know what she meant and replied,

stupidly, 'Oh no, I'll be okay. I just get depressed when we
always have to part.' She nodded. 'I mean stay with you,' she
said. 'Lie down with you.' Again I said stupidly, not knowing
what she meant, 'Okay, we can lie on the bed.' And we did,
just holding each other. And then she started giggling. I asked
'What's so funny?' And she said, 'I've never lain fully clothed
on a bed with anyone before, with my boots on into the
bargain.' Then I knew. I looked at her. 'Do you really want
to?' I asked. I didn't, myself. The feelings I had for her had
always been so singular, so intense, they had never converted
into desire for her body. But somehow I thought I should say
yes. How can you love someone and not accept the body as
well? I argued to myself. She said to me 'I think I must have
always loved you, Meg.' And got up and went to get her night
things. I lay there, with the light still on, like some clumsy
virgin, apprehensive and afraid, somehow. She came back and
undressed very matter-of-factly, so I did as well. We lay naked
together and kissed. Her passion surprised me and I couldn't
match it, though I pretended. Emotionally I was consumed by
her, but my body didn't somehow feel the same pitch. I've
faked orgasms with men but she was the first woman with
whom I've done that. I'm more ashamed of that than
anything. Somehow the situation was too rushed, too
unprepared. I couldn't understand why it had happened. I still
don't, although I'm now having guesses. Afterwards she
wanted to go back to her own bed, which disappointed me.
Being close to her was what was important. But she reassured
me and said it had been *good*, a *good* thing to do and it was
only that she wasn't very comfortable in such a small bed.
The next day was as usual — perhaps more heightened but of
the same quality as ever, which I think reassured us both that
we hadn't made a mistake or done something destructive. And
then she left. And the next week the thing with Jim
happened. I couldn't tell you this before.

We were sitting in the café and she asked what sort of
problem about Jim I meant. I didn't want to say he raped me. I
said he'd made a pass at me and that I felt I had to tell her.
She laughed. She took my hand and said, 'Is that all? Well,

don't let it worry you. It won't come between you and me. And it's not going to destroy my marriage.' I couldn't believe she was able to take it so lightly, but my heart sang just the same. All that agonising had been uneccessary. She added that she thought it would be a good idea if they didn't come and stay in our house the next time they were in London, but that otherwise it wouldn't make any difference.

So that was that. We talked about other things. I decided, therefore, to stay over and go back the next day to New York. I didn't want to see Jim, of course, and she didn't even mention it, but she said she wanted to come and have a late breakfast with me in the hotel next day, before I left. She said she'd come to my room at nine o'clock. By eleven o'clock she hadn't come or phoned so I phoned her. She was really distant and I could tell she didn't want to talk to me at all but I pressed her. Eventually she said that she'd gone home and asked Jim if it was true that he'd made a pass at me when he'd been in London. *And he'd laughed and said of course not.* So she clearly thought I'd been lying.

I couldn't believe it. I couldn't believe the change in her. I lost control. I spluttered down the phone. I said things like 'Have I ever told you any lies? Ever, ever? He bloody raped me, for God's sake. And what reason, for Christ's sake, would I have for telling a lie like this?' And *then* she said 'I thought it had something to do with what happened between us in London.' God. And she started crying and said 'I feel so *dirty*.' I started shouting that she had to believe me, that she owed it to our friendship to believe me, that I could tell her all about Jim's body if she really wanted me to — and how would she have felt having his great balls stuck in front of her nose — and how disgustingly he had talked about her and how I couldn't forgive him for that — and what she really ought to ask herself is not why *I* would tell such a lie, having no reason to bring all this on my head and possibly lose her, but why *he* would tell such a lie and how he clearly had *reason* to lie.

I still can't believe that she can't see that. If he'd said, as I unconsciously expected, that yes he'd made a pass and so what, we all could have coped with it, thought of it as an embarrassing incident that wouldn't happen again, and so life would have gone on. But his denial is proof, louder than any proof, that his real motive was the destruction of our friendship. And he has succeeded. Which leaves me open-mouthed at the injustice that we should be the victims of his egotism, greed and contempt and that she should cling to him and believe him no matter what. My God!

I persuaded her that things couldn't be left there and she cried and said okay she'd meet me and that she was glad I'd phoned because she really would have just let me go and never seen me again. I put off my meeting in New York and arranged that I would go out to the university to her room at four o'clock. Which I did. And will you believe it? When I got there, there was a *padlock* on the door. No note. No message. Nothing. I was left standing there like a fool. I can't forgive her for that, though I may one day. And so I came to New York and am trying to concentrate on the work I'm supposed to be doing but I'm really having a battle controlling myself. How could she cut me off like that? How *could* she?

Why didn't it occur to me that part of Jim's strategy would be denial? I don't feel I want revenge on him. I don't feel anything at all about him, except the utmost contempt. But I have a range of feelings about her that would cover the spectrum, if there was one for feelings. Betrayed, I suppose. Used. Manipulated and discarded.

I've been to see someone who was at college with Jim years ago. I went last night. Not about that, as it happens, but of course the subject came up. Her name's Joy. She laughed and said 'Everyone in town knows Jim is like that. He's always been like that. He's a real prick.' I asked why Frances seemed not to know. 'Well,' said Joy, 'first I suppose she doesn't want to know, and second, who is going to tell her? No one ever tells the wife and anyway he'd deny it, wouldn't he? and she'd believe him, wouldn't she? It suits her to believe him.' 'At any cost?' I asked. 'I would think so,' she said.

I suppose it's the wound to my ego I can't get over yet. That I should be so unimportant, not even worth a conversation about it, that she could drop me out of her life as if I'd never existed.

Can't do any more now. See you when I get back.

Love,
Meg

ℰ

Meg to Amy

30 July

Dear Amy,

Back again. Everything pretty bleak. No word from Frances. Suppose I shouldn't expect it. But I do. Wish I could talk to you — talk it out. Finally broke down and told Jan and practically everyone else I know. I so wish I didn't have this particular weakness, just to tell all. Never was the brave, silent type. Most of them were furious with me for not saying anything before. Oh well.

Jane *wasn't* on my doorstep when I got back, but a letter was. I enclose it. I don't know how to answer it or what to do about it. Sorry to turn you into my mother-confessor — I promise it's temporary. The rest of my life, after all, is fine; Simon is getting on well at nursery school and bringing home the odd friend (all boys though!) and my money problems have abated for a while. I don't know why I'm still in such a state about the whole Frances thing — why I can't throw it off. Life is shit-mysterious, sometimes......

It's something to do with injustice. Jim was the villain but he gets what he wanted. Frances and I were the innocent parties and we have to sacrifice our friendship. Or are we being punished by the gods for going to bed that once? Perhaps the friendship wasn't even so important to her, or she couldn't have abandoned it so easily. I'm sorry for myself today as you can see.

What shall I do about Jane?

Love,
Meg

ℰ

Jane to Meg

25 July

Dear Meg,

I've talked to Amy, including blowing my top at her about you, which I realised after was both nasty and irrelevant. Having attacked you by proxy I apologise by proxy. I was going to come down and meet your flight, or land on your doorstep, but I thought better of it. I have to do something about restraining my impulses, I can see. Other people get hurt by them, though God knows that is not my motive.

Please accept my sympathy, belated though it is, for what has happened to you. What bothered me about my own reaction, I realised later, was that it was very much like jealousy. And I don't know why. Obviously I'm quite sure I'm not jealous that you were raped. It has something to do with your hold on life. Things happen to you. Or for you. You seem to have some access to energy which I've been seeking and want for myself. Something about you makes me want to get closer to you. I can't explain it. I'm probably doing it yet again, now — writing on impulse when I ought to be more careful. But then I'd never say anything and I'd be dishonest in my own eyes. Oh hell. I hope you will know what I'm talking about.

Can I come and see you?

Love,
Jane

ह♦

Amy to Meg

5 August

Dear Meg,

Have your letter of 30 July and Jane's letter to you. About that first. Don't be too concerned. She's pretty fiery and her bark's worse that her bite. I think she's probably a real softy underneath, though I haven't had that sort of contact with her, being mostly engaged in political debates from the opposite side of the fence. She is responsive to you and I don't think you need be anxious about that.

I also haven't heard from Frances since you were there. I haven't written myself, thinking it would be better to respond to whatever she had to say than to write an artificial sort of letter as if I didn't know what has gone on — or as if you hadn't told me. But I may write now.

It seems fairly clear to me that whatever the dynamics between Jim and you and between Frances and you, the third piece of the jigsaw is whatever those two were working out about their own relationship *through you*. I know it's a hard thought, but perhaps you needn't be so personal about all this. It may be much more something Frances couldn't handle and therefore something that she could have unconsciously turned to you for. And Jim's realisation of that may have prompted him to react how he did.

Not that I excuse any of it for one minute, but it seems that for you the hardest thing is your inability to understand. I don't blame you. You don't really have enough information to be able to understand. But you have to do your best with what you've got. Frances probably can't bear to be in contact with you at the moment because you must be forcing her to face something about Jim, or about her relationship with him, which she must know underneath but which is so awful that she will do anything not to have to face it. Not very admirable, and no comfort to you, but nevertheless, very female. Part of our oppression. Our lack of self-confidence and self-esteem. And part of the way we've been conditioned to judge ourselves as if we were primarily sexual creatures, as if that were our only real value, so that if there is some threat to our sexual status quo, we are conditioned to fall apart.

Remember Frances hasn't had any experience in groups or with other intimate relationships — she's naive and therefore much more likely to be threatened by the knowledge of what Jim is really like, than you or I would be. And if she really is fond of him, that knowledge would be more or less devastating, wouldn't it? The wound in her self-image would be a severe one.

Leave her for a while — I'm sure she'll come round. Otherwise she has to face the wound in her self-image about having made a mistake about *you* all these years. She will have to be thinking, if she thinks at all, that either she's been really wrong about Jim or she's been really wrong about you — one of you is a monster. That can't be a very comfortable position to be in. Which one would you choose? She can't come and live with you, can she? We have to *politicise* these situations — help women to stop being so personal and see the symbolism of them. Chin up.

> Love,
> Amy

ॐ

Meg to Jane

9 August

Dear Jane,

Thanks for your letter. I'm not really sure what you're on about — sorry if that disappoints you, but I have to be honest as well. You scare me a bit — my alarm system is ringing. But I've been hurt recently, as you know, and I'm also wary of you because of all that stuff about boy children and so on. I think you *ought* to come and visit — despite my reservations — and see my son and how we live. I think you are somehow so involved in theory and in your own tempestuous emotions that you may find it easier, or *I* may find it easier, to solve some of these things in a life context. (That sounds stuffy, I know, but I'm not as confident as I was — my nerve's been shaken.) Let me know when you can come. There's plenty of space.

I've been thinking what it is that's so specially repulsive about rape. My male friends don't think it is all that awful, when they're honest — no more awful than being beaten up. It's the *invasion*. But they say any act of physical violence is an invasion, which is true too. I think it's the *dehumanisation* of it, which is so total, and which means that I am nothing except an object in someone else's fantasy. An extreme acting out of what women are to men. What do you think?

See you soon, perhaps?

Meg

୫

Meg to Amy

10 August

Dear Amy,

Thanks for your letter. You're so right. It has all happened before, only not so extremely. It goes on happening. My consciousness is so heightened now that I can see and feel the same experience being repeated over and over, but with less directness, less intensity and at such a refined level that much less damage gets to me.

Two weeks ago I started working with a local men's group, after seeing one of their notices in our bookshop, to enlarge the donor pool for artificial insemination which I've been helping with. The men agreed to help, since it fits in with their commitment to accountability, which I remember you writing to me about ages ago. The chap who serves as contact for the group explained their position to me and it was such a relief after some of the emotionally difficult situations I've got into elsewhere. Men have so many ways of calling upon one's female energies. Sometimes I've been in the position where a woman has requested a donation and I've arranged it for her and gone along expecting merely to collect the donation and found that instead I was being asked, in a very subtle, non-verbal way, to be pleasant and sociable and somehow grateful and reassuring. The men in this new group do not regard giving donations as doing a favour to women — they see it as another way of redressing the imbalance which makes it necessary for the woman to ask in the first place. Sperm banks and all the resources provided for infertile men's wives should be available to all women who want to choose AID.

The trauma with Jim, and the experiences over the last two

weeks with men from the group, have combined to sensitise me beyond the liberal-humanist expedience of humouring people in whatever way they seem to need so that they'll feel good. If a donor, that is, is saying 'Be nice to me and I can be nice back again', I am put into a false position of having to be nurturant and also having to be grateful if it works. It's what Wages Due Lesbians call 'emotional housekeeping' — the old providing of the breast (actual or metaphorical) for a male with a problem. I'm no longer willing — or perhaps I'm no longer able, I'm not sure which — to behave in this very female way, unless I am in a position to choose it. The way I know if it's that sort of negotiation is the resultant anger if I'm not nice. These particular men do not ask for anything in return for giving a donation — not even gratitude. *Therefore* one is quite free to be grateful.

I'm having such trouble with Jan about this. She says I am becoming over-ideological and that these kinds of demands are just the same between any two people, including any two women. But to me it isn't the same. Because a man enjoys privilege, simply because he is male, one is never really equal.

Everything is somehow coming to a head with Jan, who has been coasting along most of the time recently, showing a fairly hefty degree of boredom with my growing investment in some of the tenets of feminist practice and who is also, I suspect, more disturbed than either of us has expressed about the rape. I think she secretly thinks I somehow provoked it, or I encouraged it, or that somehow I could have stopped it if I'd really wanted to. This is very painful but I can't do anything about it. It is making me grow away from her, whether I want to or not. If reality seems so different to her, it is hard to feel close for us both. At least my relationship with Simon goes on as usual, for which I am very grateful because it gives me some strength to keep believing in my own perceptions.

Do write when you can. Meanwhile my love,

Meg

ॐ

Jane to Meg

11 August

Dear Meg,

I can come at the weekend and have managed to
borrow a car so don't worry about having to meet any trains.
I'll phone when I'm off the motorway on Friday evening just
to let you know roughly when I'll be there.

I'm looking forward very much to meeting you although I'm a
bit anxious about Simon. I don't want to hurt you, but I'm aware
that the level of my hostility towards any male is more than
most women have and I can't really apologise for it. But you
must have been aware of that possibility when you agreed
that I should come. Just wanted to be open about it.

Don't bother about making up beds and all that sort of
thing. I've got a sleeping bag and of course I want to
contribute to your housekeeping expenses. I can stay till
Monday night and will drive back Tuesday, if that's all right
with you.

See you Friday,

In sisterhood,
Jane

෧෨

Amy to Meg

14 August

Dear Meg,

Nice to have your letter. I'm worried about what you say
about Jan and you. You've been together so long — isn't it
eight or nine years? — and I feel upset at the thought of your
splitting in such a casual-sounding way. I know you didn't say
anything direct about splitting, but I sense it between the
lines and want to encourage you to sit down together and
have a good long session about all these things. Your trauma
with Jim, after all, hasn't happened to Jan. Don't be too
impatient with her. It's worth working hard on every relationship we have with each other so that the fabric of understanding can spread.

I certainly don't approve of the nuclear family, but after all
Jan has been involved in Simon's upbringing since the
beginning and you have to think of the effect on him if Jan
were to leave. God, I'm beginning to sound like some awful
marriage counsellor, but I can't help myself. I think, as well,
that it's so reminiscent of some of the stages I've been through
with Tim. Especially in the beginning. One of us was always
on the point of leaving, but fortunately for us, when those
times were happening, the other one was usually in a position
of positive emotional strength and managed to reassure the
one who was under threat. I think perhaps that's what I mean
— we somehow recognised that when we were warring like
that, it was because one of us was under some huge threat
that the other one momentarily seemed to be embodying. I
saw Tim at those times as an archetype of all men — and
couldn't bear it — and he saw me as an archetype of the
Amazon — and couldn't bear that. Usually in the end we
managed to see each other in some sort of perspective and to
thrash out most of the issues that seemed to be dividing us.

Do let me know about all this,

Love,
Amy

ॐ

Meg to Amy

20 August

Dear Amy,

I appreciate your mothering, or 'marriage-counselling' as
you so deprecatingly call it — deeply, in fact — but it's
difficult to convey in a letter the range of feelings and little
disagreements involved. Jan, for example, has never supported
my arranging inseminations for other women. Her attitude
has been something like 'if that's what they really want, they
should go somewhere proper to get it' — meaning a doctor or
a hospital. I've told her dozens of times that for these women
going to a hospital is impossible. They haven't got
connections and don't know how the profession operates and

anyway they've usually tried their own doctors first. They only come to see me as the last gasp, but I can't get her to understand that. If I say no, there's no other possibility for them so they would then have to think about picking up a casual man, with all the physical risks involved, especially VD.

When I started I was happy enough to do it alone, since we'd always had quite a lot of separate interests. I didn't think about it much. Now, though, when there seem to be increasing emotional problems of one sort or another, I'm not so willing to take on the whole thing alone and I even think I shouldn't. It's something that really needs a collective share of responsibility, counselling of the women, and money. Not to mention time. The sorts of situations which I told you about in my last letter, I couldn't keep to myself and Jan really blew her top when I turned to her for support. The trouble is, she's just not interested in feminism and therefore we always have to begin everything from the beginning. It's so frustrating.

As well as that, Jane has been here and Jan was really turned off by her! She wasn't here most of the weekend, having arranged to take Simon to see some friends. But we did all have Saturday evening together and all I can say about that is that much exhaustion and argument was had by all. Jane behaved disgracefully, losing her temper and shouting at Jan about 'women like her' and generally throwing her weight around, which, apart from anything else, was bloody rude and was also, I thought, no way to treat a 'sister'. I told her so the next day.

But Jan behaved badly too, turning on her most sulky and aggravating pose of boredom and superiority, appearing smug and self-contained in her personal little world and therefore giving the sense of being very selfish and rather stupid. And I am not guiltless either, throwing myself first on one side and then on the other and not managing to persuade anyone about anything.

Jane went back Monday evening and I've arranged to go and visit her in a month's time, when Simon is having a week in the country with his granny. No boy children (or any males) are allowed in their house! But I want to see it, just the same, and I like Jane in spite of everything. I told her she was crazy — and I mean it — but I couldn't help warming to her — she's so vital somehow.

Jan has been in a sulk ever since Jane left and I'm so fed up with it that I can't be bothered trying to pull her out of it. I appreciate what you're saying about all the work one has to do to keep a relationship good and functioning, but I've lost the impetus with Jan. I'm somewhere else. We're not on the same planet. Except with regard to Simon, as you say. She loves him, and he loves her too, and that won't change, whatever happens between her and me.

I always said, right from the beginning, that the child should make his own relationships with the people around him and that I wouldn't interfere with them, unless there seemed to be something negative happening, and I stick to that. I really believe it's the only way. That we have to attack the Bowlby myth effectively, by showing that children do *not* have to find mother the all-powerful and only important person in their infant universe and that the best way to free women from all this guilt and to encourage them to get out of the maternal house is to bring up children to have multiple primary relationships.

I think it's especially important for male children, to combat this heavy conditioning they bring to their adult life where they are always on the lookout for a holy madonna to nourish them, along with their children, while it leaves them free to range wide and sleep with anyone they fancy. It's not just that they suffer, all of them, from madonna-whore syndrome — it's that we keep behaving as if we are either madonnas or whores (or both, alternately), to different men. So Simon will keep his bond with Jan, even if she does move out, or even if Simon and I do. I'm even prepared to think about his living with her, if that seems best for him, though it would cause me the most frightful anguish.

I think, with all due respect, that we have been less of a

nuclear family than you and Tim have been, simply because the social perception of two women together is different from that of the heterosexual model. If you and Tim lived communally with others it might appear different, but you don't. Even though you explain your relationship with him so carefully and explicitly, he still seems to me to be your husband rather than your lover, whereas Jan seems to be either my lover or my friend. We don't have a 'marital' relationship.

I must go. Lots to do. Still no word from Frances.

Love,
Meg

P.S. I've just thought that there are things you don't know about Jan and me. Yes, we have been together a long time — but you shouldn't assume from that that we're pledged to stay together for ever. I think lesbians know better than heterosexual women the vulnerability and transience of connection.

Jan and I met when each of us had just broken from a relationship. It was all years ago, before we'd heard of feminism. In the days when two women never admitted 'living together' except to a chosen few friends. When we each kept up separate bedrooms and went to other people's parties expecting to be provided with men. I don't think we ever danced with one another until we went, years later, to a women's disco for the first time.

I'm sorry, Amy. You'll think this very unsisterly of me, but I really think you can't know what it's like to sustain a relationship in almost complete secrecy, with guilt and a sense of being unclean having to be fought down all the time. We lived like that. For years. So you see, if the passion has gone cold and we're talking about separating, it isn't full of rage and revenge like people getting a divorce. We've been through so much together, have given each other so much support, know each other so intimately, that we will always be part of one another, whatever happens. It doesn't need saying between us. Doesn't need proving. We both need a change. But the hurt you mean just isn't there in the way you think. Just sadness that nothing lasts.

Love again,
Meg

ॐ

Meg to Jane   20 August

Dear Jane,

Have just written to Amy but really wanted to be writing to you so I may as well. I must tell you how different you are from what I had expected. I had an image in my mind, built up through your letters. You are so blood-and-thunder on paper. I had conjured up a woman with close cropped hair, blazing eyes, overalls one or two sizes too large, heavy walking boots and a stocky frame. Imagine my shock when I opened the door and saw you for real — long blonde hair hanging loose, a tall, slim body with immaculate trousers and a silk blouse, and that very smart scarf tied close into the throat. And your long slender fingers, so deft and capable, were the biggest surprise of all. You never said you could sew! I can't get that image out of my mind — it has made such an impression on me and somehow magically made your words seem softer than they are, because you have such a look of softness about you. You'll hate me for this, but you seemed so quintessentially feminine — so capable of tenderness and gentleness. Now if I'm not careful I shall wax poetic and embarrass us both, as well as infuriating you, since the mental counterpart of my image of you is that you very much don't want to appear soft and gentle — that you would regard that as some kind of silly weakness.

I want to say too how very much I enjoyed your visit, apart from the fracas on Saturday night with Jan — to whom you were perfectly horrible, you know. I wish it hadn't happened. She's been sulking all week about it in a sort of implacable way so that I haven't the energy (or is it the motivation?) to get her out of it. Neither of you did justice to yourselves. She is really an exceptionally nice person — no one could be nicer, for example, when one is ill or in trouble. She is kind, patient and sympathetic, as well as being practical and competent.

I'm having trouble lately because she is, for some reason, more and more opposed to feminism — or to my involvement with feminism — and I somehow can't handle it. We are becoming gradually more separate and distant, apart from our mutual caring for Simon. We've been together so long and we know each other's moods so well that I haven't the heart to go on attacking her position, especially when I suspect that some part of it at least is a jealous reaction of some kind to my getting more involved with things and people than I used to be.

Thanks for what you said about Frances. I didn't expect that you would be so understanding about it, but when you told me about your friendship with Susan and what had happened to it, I could see how you would know what was so painful to me. Is it always like that? Are men really so powerful that they can go on breaking up important relationships between women? Or is it that women really are so weak that they can't prevent it happening? I hate the whole idea.

I'm looking forward to seeing you next month. Meanwhile, take care —

Love,
Meg

ॐ

Jane to Meg

26 August ·

Dear Meg,

So good to have your letter. I enjoyed meeting you too — enormously — but it's no good pretending I enjoyed meeting Jan. I've never understood how a woman can live a lesbian life and not be a feminist. She seemed so intractably opposed to everything that to me is self-evident — it was like trying to argue with someone out of the Ark, or out of the caves. I don't want to hurt your feelings, but I may as well be honest about it. Since you're so stubborn about bringing up a boy child, I think you should have a very intense session with yourself about what sort of result you are bound to have if you allow him to have such a close exposure to thinking like Jan's.

It's not good, Meg, having fantasies about a universal sisterhood. If there is such a thing it is general rather than particular, and does not prevent individual women from disliking each other or from having serious conflicts. We manage to keep most of those conflicts to ourselves, which is relatively easy while we are so embattled and relatively powerless, but it won't always be like that. Women like Jan will have to choose which side they're on — and if they choose to play Uncle Tom they will have to cope with the consequences.

I, for one, am not afraid to express my rage towards anyone who opposes our liberation — it is our right, it is the way to future health, and it is worth total commitment. I won't see it obstructed, not willingly, anyway, even if I have to fight friends and lovers of my own friends and lovers. Yes, I was rude. I meant to be. How else can one get through such an obstinate ostrich act? Gentle persuasion doesn't work. It ends up in manipulation, guilt, evasion and politeness and that's a waste of time and energy. So don't ask me to apologise — I won't. I don't think I even should. I don't deny there might have been an element of personal jealousy involved — on both our parts — but I don't apologise about that either. I like you and want to know you better, and if one likes someone one doesn't want to see that person diminished by connections with less worthy people. You can't defend a relationship between unequals to me — I've seen too much of it and too many women misusing their energies and talents because of it. People grow and people change and one has to have the courage to move on. Oh, I know you'll think this is brutal and nasty of me, but you're somewhere else, Meg, and you'll have to accept that, painful though it is.

Glad you liked my clothes. You must have forgotten that I was a docile wife for some years and of course that meant

being able to sew and being able to choose clothes which
showed off one's best advantages. Not the sort of habit it's
easy to get rid of, and I haven't thought, till now, that I
should. But you're right — I don't like seeming to be
'quintessentially feminine'. You should know better than to
call any feminist 'feminine' — it has such a media-gloss
meaning. But I forgive you this once, since you mean to
compliment me and I shouldn't be such a prig that I can never
be graceful about anything.

Very much looking forward to seeing you when you come.
Our house is relatively peaceful at the moment — the
council has agreed to give us an extension, so the money
pressure is off for a while. Every time we're getting close to
the breadline there's the most almighty outbreak of emotional
problems. It would be so easy not to be 'hysterical' and
'neurotic' if we had enough money to live on without having
to plan all the time. Why should men have all the money?

> In sisterhood,
> Jane

ଚ୶

Meg to Jane

30 August

Dear Jane,

God, you are a beast about poor Jan! Who gave you the right
to be her judge and mentor? She hasn't harmed you, and it
wouldn't do you any damage to show some compassion. You
haven't had to grow up lesbian, and that makes a lot of
difference. Adolescence is such a vulnerable time, and if there
was little or no support then, it is understandable that a
woman might be permanently weakened and not *ever* able to
be as confident of her identity as you are. You were in the
mainstream all the time — you've never had to prove yourself
on your own. You've done it all — learned to play the female
role, been married and so on. The fact that you rebel against it
all now is not all that amazing, is it?

I don't mean to suggest you haven't been hurt — or that you

haven't had a tough time with your husband. But you *have* had something Jan has never had — implicit social approval and support. You should know all this. Can't you be more 'graceful', as you put it? Can't you see that someone like Jan knows more about the real experience of lesbianism in a patriarchy than you ever can? that her still-forming personality was irrevocably bruised by the abuse she had to contend with?

I think it's amazing that she was ever able to love anyone at all, and the love she shows Simon is caring, healthy and good. I won't have you saying such things. Simon is a very lucky child to have someone like Jan parenting him. Even if we do split up, I shall make sure that that relationship is disturbed as little as possible.

I feel so angry with you that I almost don't care whether I ever see you again or ever hear from you again if you are really as intolerant and arrogant as your letter is. Did you keep a copy of it? Why don't you have another look at what you wrote. As for being jealous, that is no excuse for the things you said, and if you mean jealous on my account, I'm not interested. Yes, I'm having trouble in my relationship with Jan at the moment, but that is really none of your business and anyway doesn't mean I'm on the lookout for another lover. I'm so exasperated with you. Why should you have this sort of outrageous persecuting attitude towards Jan, just because she doesn't agree with you? Who gives you the right? Who?

I was so much looking forward to coming to visit you and and seeing your house and meeting the women you've described. . . but now I've had your letter, I'm not sure whether I want to any more. Oh Jane, don't turn feminism into yet another bloodthirsty religion, full of punishment and revenge and dogma and the saved and the unsaved. Haven't we had enough of that from men?

In 'sisterhood',
Meg

Jane to Meg

3 September

Dear Meg,

I see I've gone off the deep end again. No, I don't keep copies of my letters, but judging from yours, mine must have been much more aggressive than I remember. I still think I have a right to my anger and my principles, but I must agree with you that I haven't an unlimited right to shed them forth on an ungrateful public. Seriously, I've read and re-read your letter and in the end can see that it's full of righteous indignation, so I must have been much too fierce. Please understand how hard it is for some of us to be confronted with anti-feminist sentiment when we're investing everything in making feminism work. You're right though — male religion has been responsible for hideous persecutions, and I respect you enough to take notice if you say I remind you of that sort of perversion.

I do apologise for having hurt your feelings and for being too aggressive and if you want me to grovel, I will.

Something in what you said interests me very much. We didn't really talk about it while I was with you, but I'd like to know more about it. It's the point about growing up lesbian. I don't know much about that, as all the women in my house are political lesbians who haven't had the sort of experience you describe. Perhaps you could tell me more about it when you write again. (Do please write again — and do please come and visit as we arranged. I'm sorry if what I said was too strong. It's a common complaint about me.)

People living in a politically charged atmosphere are not always in touch with what is going on outside, and perhaps are specially liable to become enraged when faced with apathy. But surely even you can't really approve of Jan's particular stance? Do write anyway.

In sisterhood,
Jane

Meg to Jane

8 September

Dear Jane,

Well, I'm writing to you again, against my better judgement. There *is* something charming about you, in spite of your beastliness. I can still see you on my doorstep — can still see you cross-legged by my fire, looking for all the world like a sultry blonde in a television commercial. I can't help it, but that keeps modifying my exasperation. The discord keeps clanging in my ears — your language and opinions just don't match with your external image. I've never been so confronted with this kind of disjunction before. Have you heard the same thing from other friends? I'd be interested to know.

Look, I have to lecture you about toning down your tongue and not thinking that saying exactly what you think is the same thing as being honest. Being honest means *carefully* sifting through one's welter of feelings and perceptions, *including other people's feedback*, and then arriving at a stage where you really do know what you think. It doesn't mean just holding forth at the drop of a hat. Feminism shouldn't be used as an excuse to be a bully. Whatever men, or your husband, did to you, however much they bullied you, is not a reason for you to go about bullying other women. Please think about this.

As to your question: growing up lesbian means never being able to belong to the peer group, at a time when it is more important to belong than at any other stage in one's life. Other friends are having feelings which one doesn't seem to have oneself, and nothing is more likely to induce depression, feelings of inadequacy and loss of confidence. As well as that, there is the dilemma about sexuality — what sort one has (since there is no one to give any guidance) and what to do with it.

When I was young, for example, and my mother found love-letters from my first female partner, the consequences were so different from what happened to my girl friends who were dating boys for the first time. In their case, their mothers were so proud and supporting — they boasted to other mothers about their daughters — they bought them clothes and make-up and hair-dos — they arranged parties for them — and so on. I know feminists are against all that and it wouldn't perhaps happen the same way now — but the point is that these 'heterosexual' girls were being given positive encouragement and were constantly being told they were okay. In my case, in Jan's case, in anyone's case who grew up lesbian, mother (and father) were horrified. In place of encouragement came blame, regret, anxiety and a host of other reactions which could do nothing except evoke the most extreme sense of guilt in the young girl.

My mother (supported by my father) first took away the letters, then made me see a doctor (the first of many) and then insisted that I join a local church fellowship (mixed) and a dancing class (also mixed). The latter was pure torture. Learning the heterosexual flirting games, competing with other girls for boys I didn't really want, dressing up in clothes I didn't like, pretending to be stupid when I wasn't — the whole thing was a nightmare. I tried. Very hard. No one at that age really wants to be different or has strong principles about what it all means. All one does is fight for survival — one fights to be included, to be thought well of, to be like everyone else. Well, lesbian girls are *not* like anyone else. They have intensely passionate love affairs that spring straight from the centre of themselves (having no other models or external patterns to follow) — and because the emotions feel so honest and true, nothing from the external world can shift them. I remember these silly doctors saying things like 'It's natural enough, dear, at this stage, but soon you'll meet a nice boy' or 'You should get out and meet more people and not take yourself so seriously' — and so on.

Don't you see how different it was for you? and for the women in your house? You have grown up being one of the accepted ones. You have proved your womanhood in society's terms. The fact that you have later rejected it is not really important to the outside. They can see it as some sort of temporary aberration, or some mad piece of muddled political ideology which they don't have to take seriously. You *must* secretly like men really, because you've been married and had boyfriends. You're not one of those sick, disturbed females who have consistently preferred their own sex as friends and sexual partners. Your political choice to live as a lesbian is exactly that — political. It just isn't so threatening as natural homosexuality. You can be *seen* to have made a choice and it is easy enough for society to shrug it off as the wrong choice.

Women like Jan and myself are not seen like that — and were specially not seen like that when we were young. We were treated as different, abnormal and nasty. It is not surprising, therefore, for a woman like Jan to grow up nursing her guilty secret and being shy of parading the very thing that has always caused pity, contempt or punishment. Have a bit more imagination and you won't then be so relentlessly idealistic. Your sort of idealism turns easily enough into cruelty.

It's easier for me than for Jan. I'm more extraverted and more dominating and have always rebelled against the social opprobrium I've encountered. She is quieter and gentler, easier to hurt, more vulnerable to cruelty, more warm-hearted and kind than I am. I have been more cunning, more expedient, less honest, more aggressive — I have used any survival tools I had. Jan is not such a fighter. Why should she be? Women like you, who have not been so damaged as she was, should be leading a campaign for proper sex education, for instance, so that all the new generations of Jans need not grow up in this frightful way. Do that — don't condemn her.

Must go now. Simon is about to descend from school, with God knows how many little friends who will all want milk and cakes. No doubt they'll be your favorite brand of humanity — little boys. I've yet to feel any more oppressed by them than I do by a bunch of little girls, who also spill milk on the carpet and hide cakes in the linen drawers. The boys, certainly, are more prone to have gunfights and wrestle with each other — but they see all that on television, don't they? My not having a son won't change that. And if he were someone else's son, he might be getting active encouragement to behave like that. Don't dream big dreams. See what is possible and support that.

I send you my love — as I said, in spite of myself.

Meg

ॐ

Jane to Meg

15 September

Dear Meg,

Thank you for your long letter and your words of wisdom. I took the liberty of reading it out to the other women in the house and we had a long discussion about what you wrote. We agreed that you're right about one thing at least — that we could try to get involved in sex education in some of our local schools. Betty, the woman with the most time to spare at the moment, has agreed to sus this out and report back on the possibilities.

I'm still politically opposed to male children. But having met Simon, who is not as bad as some, it is difficult to consign him to some unknown fate and maybe you're right, that he's better off with you than he would be somewhere else. The answer, of course, is not to have them at all, but since he exists, I suppose some accommodation has to be made. What you're really telling me is that it's not always possible to live strictly according to principles — a thought which I find profoundly depressing but is no doubt true. I'll write again soon.

Love,
Jane

ॐ

Amy to Frances

15 September

Dear Frances,

I haven't heard from you for such a long time — an absolute
age, in fact. Are you all right? I don't have vibes that you're
not all right, but I wonder why you haven't written?

I haven't heard from Meg lately either and can't see when I
would be able to make enough space to go and visit her. I
know our mutual friend Jane has been down, but I haven't
heard from Jane either. No one seems to want to write to me
any more! Do let me know how you are.

Love,
Amy

ઠ

Frances to Amy

25 September

Dear Amy,

I have your letter of 15 September, which I've been debating
whether to answer or not. In the end I decided it wasn't quite
fair simply to disappear without any sort of explanation, but
after what has happened with Meg I can't and won't entertain
the idea of getting any more involved in all this pernicious,
trouble-making nonsense. It seems to have ruined my
most important friendship, not to mention making waves in
my marriage.

I don't know if your letter is ingenuous, or whether Meg
really has said nothing to you about what happened. I somehow
can't believe she wouldn't. She was never one for keeping
things to herself.

I've settled down with a cup of coffee, a free morning, a pile
of Meg's old letters to me, a cat curled up on the armchair
and a head full of confusion, resolved to get it all down on
paper somehow. I intended to do that anyway, but the whole
thing was so awful I didn't have the heart. At least your letter
provided both the stimulus and the motivation and I thank

you for that. I must admit, nevertheless, that because you're a
friend of Meg's I can hardly see you as an objective person and
don't know at all whether you will believe what I say.

I met Meg in our old café, as planned. I had the usual
excitement and looking-forward feelings which meeting her
always brought up in me, whatever 'low' I might be having.
Imagine my dismay, therefore, when she broke down and told
me Jim had made a pass at her. I didn't let on, I think, what a
jolt it gave me, and comforted her and said it didn't matter. In
a way, it didn't. Our relationship has always been extremely
important to both of us (*had* been, I should say), and
somehow intact and apart from anything else. Likewise I have
kept my marriage intact and apart. And I know Jim. He's
rather conceited and has a jokey social manner and he may
have teased Meg in some way she didn't like, being lesbian,
and which she misinterpreted. I didn't like the thought, but it
didn't seem all that serious and I suggested we just didn't stay
with her again when we were in London.

When I got home I asked Jim about it and said Meg had
been upset. He flatly denied the whole thing. He said 'Don't
be ridiculous. Meg is having fantasies' and things like that. I
decided I didn't want to see Meg again, even though we'd
arranged another meeting. I just felt I couldn't handle it. She
is so intense, so sensitised — I now think over-sensitised — to
what I feel and say, that I knew she would know I didn't quite
believe her. And I didn't want to have to defend Jim to her.

Anyway, she phoned and persuaded me to meet,
although I had decided not to. She lost control of herself. It
was hideous. Horrible. She said the most obscene, disgusting
things about Jim — worse than any porn I've read. And full of
hatred. I thought she had gone mad. I think she must be mad.
I remember a school-friend of hers, years and years ago, when
we first knew each other, saying to me 'Be careful with Meg.
She's very clever and she seems very nice, but she's a mess
inside'.

Well, after all this long, foolish time, I see that I should
have listened. Meg said Jim had *raped* her — which is miles
worse than saying he made a pass — and she didn't say *rape* at

all when we were sitting in the café. I refuse to entertain the possibility. Jim is my *husband*. How *dare* she think she can say a thing like that and get away with it. I was so upset I went to talk to a friend of his, who has known him for a very long time. I asked whether he thought it was remotely possible. And his friend said of course not. That's what I think myself. How *could* she?

I told you that when I was in London Meg and I spent a night together. I think that must be the reason. I never want to know any lesbians, ever again. It is some sort of dreadful sickness. It must be. The fact that I slept with her must have generated huge fantasies — God knows what about — of living together, of my leaving Jim, oh, frightful things.

Anyway, I can't bear any of it and I've decided to have nothing to do with her, ever again. She can perpetrate her madness on someone else. I'm sorry I ever knew her, sorry I was ever her friend, sorry I trusted her, and sorriest of all that I gave her my body. I was such an idealistic fool, thinking how much better it would be if this last constraint were abandoned. I thought it would bring us closer. And instead, it has caused all this destruction and havoc.

If this is the sort of thing feminism produces, you can have it. I don't want to know. I want to get on with my work, live my life, protect my marriage, have decent friends, and feel clean. Life is hard enough without this sort of thing. Please do understand.

> My best wishes to
> you,
> Frances

ॐ

Amy to Frances

30 September

Dear Frances,

Thanks for your letter. I can't let stand what you have written and not make my comment about it. You're intelligent. Why not use your brains on the material you have presented and see what it all really means? I'm sorry to be cross, but I really can't stand silently by while you malign Meg the way you have, when she has not deserved it, and has anyway been through the most appalling experience any woman can imagine. The fact that she endured rape at the hands of your husband should evoke your sympathy, not your condemnation.

Rape, after all, is a political crime. It is committed by the superior class and suffered by the inferior class. All men are potentially capable of rape. It has nothing to do with sexual drive, adequacy, prowess or anything else — it is simply and merely the exertion of power. *That* is what Jim did to Meg. He made her aware, in the way most bereft of ambiguity, of his male power. She, because of fear and powerlessness, was forced to submit to it. I have also been raped. And I can tell you, if you can't imagine it for yourself, that it is the most degrading, humiliating and disgusting experience any woman can contemplate. You perhaps wouldn't be half so hard, whatever you think, if it had been done to you.

I'll be honest with you. Yes, my letter was ingenuous. Meg did not keep the whole thing to herself — no woman should be expected to. She has been put in the most invidious position. If she had gone to the police, they wouldn't have believed her. She *had* to tell you — much as it would have been easier not to. She knows well enough — we all do — that the wife is usually the last to find out, if at all. You really should ask yourself why Meg would tell such a destructive lie, and risk losing your friendship, which has been so important to her. Don't come up with that nonsense about sleeping together. If you feel guilty about that, that's your problem, not Meg's. There is no sense at all in thinking it would make Meg invent a rape. She's used to sleeping with women, after all. Why should it produce that effect?

You're grasping at straws, Frances, and you must know you are. If Jim is unfaithful, you must know, even if unconsciously. That is something all women know about their men. Meg, anyway, has been told by a woman who has known Jim for a long time that he sleeps around and that

everyone knows it. If you don't, it's because you don't want
to. Understandable, but not truthful, on your part.

Are you really willing to sacrifice Meg on the altar of Jim's
conceit? Can't you see how jealous he must have been of your
friendship to need to destroy it? Haven't you said yourself that
he's like a child? A child who will do anything he can to get
away with what he wants. And what Jim clearly wants is you
— totally and completely dependent on him. Not you as a
willing equal, but you trapped. If he dies, disappears, goes off
with another woman — what will happen to you? Nothing is
forever, much as you might wish it were.

Another thing. You *owe* it to Jim — if you care about him
at all — and you *owe* it to nameless other women, to make as
sure as you can that he doesn't do this kind of thing again. I
live with a man myself, as you know. I'm not crying for their
blood. I don't want all rapists castrated, or anything like that.
But I want men persuaded, directed, *forced* — if necessary —
to face the consequences of patriarchy and the results of their
sexism and grow up. I want a civilised society in which
women like Meg are safe and respected. In which a person's
autonomy is upheld by women and men alike. If Jim had
committed murder, would you bury your head in the sand
like this? If you go on building your sense of security on such
false foundations, you are going to get hurt in the end — badly
hurt. Meg cared enough about you to tell you the truth. To
disbelieve her in such a ruthless way is sheer cowardice and
— worse — betrayal.

I suppose you won't want to answer this. I suppose you
haven't wanted to read a word of it. But I hope you will think
over what I've said. I hope most of all that you will at least
acknowledge Meg's existence and humanity by writing to her
eventually. Injustices surface in the end.

These are hard words. I wouldn't bother writing them,
nevertheless, if I didn't care about you.

Love,
Amy

Meg to Amy

2 October

Dear Amy,

I feel so out of touch with you. With everyone, actually. Still no word from Frances. That's pretty clear at least. She must have decided once and for all that I am the monster, that Jim is a saint, and that she wants to forget she ever knew me. It's hard, but there is some comfort in the truth, all the same. She can't have been the person I thought she was. I must have been mistaken all the time. Bad for my ego, but good to find out the truth in the end. I can't wish her any harm — she's got that already, living with the awful bastard. I'll be more careful next time I think I've made a friend.

Jan has moved out. She left a week ago. I've spent the whole time musing and brooding and not being able to find out what I really feel. The house seems so empty without her. I feel lonely and depressed and lethargic. Nevertheless, there is also a sense of relief. We had got to the stage of arguing about every little thing, which was exhausting and very bad for Simon, who would watch and listen and then become very aggressive with both of us. I think it was Simon's reaction which made her do something positive in the end.

She says she hasn't left for ever, and it was all quite amicable. She says she wants to be by herself for a bit, sort things out in her head, all that kind of thing. And that it would give me a chance to do the same. Is this how things end? No great scenes, no throwing things, no tears, no helpless pleading and murderous intent? She just packed a case, gave me a phone number where she'd be, told Simon she was going away for a bit, and that was that. We've been together for such an age that it's hard readjusting to her non-presence, if you know what I mean. If feminism is causing me to lose all my important relationships, then it *must* be a religion! Isn't that what religion always does?

Seriously, though — I wish I could see you. I feel in such a mess about my life at the moment. Not sure which direction I'm heading in. I'm grieving for Frances and yet feel grateful to have found out that she's like she is. I'm lonely for Jan, but at the same time relieved not to have the constant confrontation that had been going on for so long. I'm fantasising about the possibilities Jane represents, having got to know her much better when she visited – all that about a communal life-style and so on. She doesn't seem nearly so fanatical in the flesh as she does on paper. What do you think that means?

Compared to mine you seem to have such a steady life at the moment. Do you think you could make some time for me if I came for a couple of days after seeing Jane? I'm due there the weekend after this one coming. Let me know one way or the other, please.

> Meanwhile my love,
> Meg

Jane to Meg

2 October

Dear Meg,

Are you still coming? One of the other women also wants to have a friend stay over and we're thinking about beds and so on. Can you let me know for certain?

Nothing is happening on the sex education front. All the schools are horrified at the thought of homosexuality being included in the programme as a valid alternative to hetero-sexuality. Betty is incensed by the whole thing and has started writing letters to everyone, from the MPs and councillors downwards. Bunch of bloody hypocrites, anyway. There are dozens of gays in the House of Commons – why don't they do something for these kids? That's men for you. Hypocrites and turds. It was a lesbian who came out in Parliament, wasn't it? Not a bloody male.

I can't be bothered with all that – but Betty won't be deflected and if she wants to batter her head against that particular brick wall, why stop her? It's all so hopeless. I feel we're in some terminal state of present society. People only care about themselves. As for the Bomb, women, blacks, gays and so on, they may as well drop the bomb, or execute the misfits, for all these bastard liberals would care. You could commit hara-kiri in the street and they wouldn't give a shit.

Sorry to be what you call negative. But Meg, it's all such a battle and what for? Just to get cheated and abused and spat upon or ignored. I feel so angry all the time and I can't believe in anything. I'm having a bad patch. I'll probably be all right when you're here. You're so irritatingly cheerful and such an optimist. It makes me feel better in spite of my own cynicism. I'm sure you'll cheer up all the others too when you come, although they'll probably shout at you about your recidivist liberalism. Don't worry, I won't let them savage you too much! Let me know about your coming, anyway.

> Love and sisterhood,
> Jane

ॐ

Amy to Meg

9 October

Dear Meg,
This is very rushed. Just to say of course you can come for a couple of days. It will be so good to see you. Just arrive.

> Love,
> Amy

ॐ

Meg to Jane

10 October

Dear Jane,
Sorry to be mean, but I put off making a decision about coming or not till I heard from Amy. I want to go and see her as well. It's such a long journey that I feel better if I can kill two birds. Don't worry about beds — I can sleep on the floor if necessary, and I've got a sleeping bag.

Simon is going to Jan while I'm away. She moved out a couple of weeks ago and I'm feeling very strange about it. We've been together for nearly ten years and it's rather as if someone had died, not having her around, in spite of all the arguments and problems we've had recently. It's all very friendly and civilised — we talk on the phone, are fixing up our financial affairs, all that sort of death-making activity. We hadn't really had a passionate sexual relationship for a long time — that had just faded out and not seemed important — but the domestic partnership was well established and I feel very lonely doing everything by myself. She says she feels the same, but she still thinks it's better for us to live apart, at least for a while.

I haven't heard at all from Frances. I suppose I'm coming to despise her — first, for living with such a bastard, but secondly for being such a coward and just dropping me like a hot cake. That's how adolescents behave — not grown adults. Oh well. . . .

Do cheer up. You're so hectic — either breathing fire and brimstone or mouthing gloom and despair. Neither condition is really honest, you know. See you at the weekend.

Love,
Meg

ॐ

Meg to Amy

20 October

Dear Amy,

I got back okay and have sat straight down to write to you. My head is in such a whirl and it was so good, so very good, to talk to you and see you. Thank you. I'm more grateful than you know. You give out such calm and confidence. It's so helpful.

I'm glad you showed me Frances' letter. God, what a poor fool she is. I don't blame you at all for laying into her — someone should — but I doubt if she'll take any notice. More fool her. When Jim finally does her in good and proper, which he's bound to do in the end, she'll have nothing and no one, which isn't a nice prospect. But the remedy is in her hands, no one else's. I'm glad I'm not heterosexual. I shall never have such a high degree of investment in the System that I shall lay myself open to being destroyed, in the way she is doing by protecting that cancerous marriage. As for him, he isn't worth even wasting a vengeful thought on. C'est la vie.

What I really want to write about is seeing Jane. You know I was going to pop in for a chat after leaving you. Well, I did. And ended up staying the night. Have just rushed back down the motorway, collected Simon, paid some bills and sat down here, before even sorting out the washing. I'm behaving like some giddy young girl who is nothing but a web of impulse and irresponsibility. I'm supposed to be a sober mother and reliable friend, sorting out details about the house and Jan and Simon, but what's really happening is a set of fantasies about joining Jane's household! There — I've said it. Don't be horrified — but they're all really nice and are doing something really important.

It is all mostly just fantasy, and due in part to my lapping up the human company after feeling so alone since Jan left, rattling round in this house. There's Simon, of course, but it's not the same as having adult company to share things with. Jane's household positively hums by comparison — they're all so busy getting a protest organized about the lack of proper sex education in schools. As well as all that, there's the normal money-earning and housework, but it seems so much easier when there are more to share it. I began to think we should all be living like they do — if women really are to become liberated from the full-time work of caring for house and children (usually in that order), the only way to do it seems to be to share it out. Anyway, I know I can't be serious about it because they would never agree to having Simon, and I don't want to give him up, even though I know Jan would take him like a shot. We discussed it, but both felt he should stay with me — at least for the moment.

Jane is such a strange mixture — a creature of moods and impulses on the one hand, and a determined hard-liner on the other. I told her that her indulgence in extreme mood changes was exactly the kind of characteristic people describe as 'feminine'. Doctors and the so-called helping professions are always describing women as hysterical and neurotic, and I

told Jane (though she didn't want to hear it) that carrying on
as she does simply adds fuel to the prejudice. She was pretty
quiet for a while after that conversation and I think some of it
may have sunk in.

Nevertheless, I find her so attractive and even think I may
be half in love with her. It's fairly obvious that something
similar has happened to her, though how she would describe
it I can't imagine, since she vehemently denies that there is
any such thing as 'falling in love' — says it's a load of
bourgeois crap and invented by the patriarchy to keep women
enslaved to ideals and dreams instead of encouraging them to
live more actively. I suppose it's some variation on the
Marxist argument about religion, and she may be right, for all
I know.

But I think no one can totally escape the process of cultural
conditioning, so whether being in love is mere conditioning or
whether it is some truthful human experience is a merely
academic question, since there is no one enough outside the
culture to answer it. What I think privately is that she may
never have been in love at all, not seriously — and if that is
the case, I feel sorry for her, because it will hit her harder than
most.

I'm just speculating about all this. What is not speculation
is the degree to which she fascinates me. I suppose you won't
approve, but I can't help it. It's such an age since I felt
passionate about Jan that I'm ready — I must be — for that
sort of experience to happen again.

It was super to see you and chat. Look after yourself and
don't work too hard. Whether you have six hours' sleep or
eight is not likely to change anything.

> Love,
> Meg

છે

Meg to Jane

20 October

Dear Jane,

Can't resist writing to you immediately — well, almost,

since I've just got off a letter to Amy. Why don't you go and see her soon? It seemed to me when I was with her that she's getting a bit run down and could do with some morale-boosting herself. She has to give it to other women most of the time and must need some recharging from time to time. She's such a *civilised* person — I've become enormously fond of her and think we should look after her. My less virtuous motive is that I'd like you two to be good friends, since I like you both. It's pleasant if one's friends are also friends with each other.

I must say your household fairly knocked me sideways and set me on the path of fantasy. What would it be like if I lived there too? Don't take fright — I'm only pretending. I know I couldn't do it, if for no other reason than that I'm totally unwilling to think of giving up Simon. And I know some of the attraction was simply the companionship after being alone here since Jan left. Then, too,there is the attraction of your fiery personality, which I find both stimulating and exasperating at the same time. There are some things you seem to be much wiser about than anyone I know, but others where you are so naive and pig-headed it's not true. The time I spent with you just raced by, and now I'm back here feeling as if I've only just left. Now of course I want to plan when I can come again! or at least persuade you to come and visit me. Being realistic about it, I couldn't get away anyway for another six weeks at the earliest.

Do write, all the same. I want to know what you're doing and thinking and I want to imagine you (but not in one of your tantrums) doing all that work with women which I am cut off from. What you do needs a base of more than one person. I do the inseminations and I write a lot, but that's about it, apart from arguing with the mothers of Simon's friends. . . .

Take care,
Meg

Jane to Meg

25 October

My dear Meg,

What a nice letter! I miss you already, and your letter made me miss you more. I don't know what you've done to me, but whatever it is, it's pretty powerful. I feel rather strange. Ecstatically happy and full of energy one minute and full of gloom the next — but whichever it is, it's focused round you. I want very much to see you again and talk and just be with you. I don't think I've ever before formed a bond with someone so quickly and easily. And I don't approve of myself! I think a lot of your ideas are really reactionary and that a lot of what you do is somehow tainted with bourgeois upbringing and I would like to fight you about all these things and win. And yet I don't want to fight you. You're so charming, engaging — I don't know how to put it — so *attractive* generally. I have such a muddle of feelings about it — wanting to educate you, wanting to protect you, wanting to laugh with you and share things — silly little things as well as all the women's work we do. God, this all sounds so sentimental, I'm ashamed of myself and won't write any more of it.

Glad you liked the others and the house. Do fantasise, by all means, about joining us, but you're quite right about that being absolutely out so long as you're living with your son. That's one rule we would never change. You might as well try and storm a nunnery with him. Do write back soon and meanwhile keep cheeful,

Love and sisterhood,
Jane

ॐ

Amy to Meg

27 October

Dear Meg,

Thanks for your letter — a nice surprise after meeting so soon. You gave me a lot of energy, for which much thanks.

You're right — I don't notice sometimes how drained I'm getting, especially when Tim's away and not telling me to take it easy. But talking with you has helped a lot and I've had a new set of resources to draw on this week. I wish you could have stayed longer, but maybe next time.

I'm slightly uneasy about your Jane-fixation. Be careful, Meg. Now I'm going to sound like a Great Aunt Gertrude, but are you sure you're not just susceptible at the moment to either a Frances-substitute or a Jan-substitute? Or worse, both? You've had a rough time emotionally recently and that always leaves people more vulnerable and naked than usual and it's just when you can easily enough get too quickly involved with someone new. Jane is the last person to impose any sorts of restraints on something like that, so it's up to you to be reasonable and not get into something which might hurt you even more than you've been hurt already.

I can understand your feeling lonely after all that has happened, but be a grown woman and bear it, for Simon's sake, if for no other reason. I don't really think you'd seriously consider leaving him, but if you let your emotions run away with you, you might not be able to stop yourself and that would be terribly bad for him. Jane's household is not all heaven, you know — they have all suffered quite badly one way and another and quite often have scenes, almost as bad as group therapy gone wild. They think it's all right to allow that, that it's part of their necessary healing process, and that they can be more help to each other in that way than any orthodox psychological services could be. I'm more cautious, as you know, and find this sort of acting out rather frightening. It would certainly not be a helpful environment to take Simon into, even if they would allow it. I'm sure they wouldn't, by the way, so as long as all this dreaming stays in your imagination I suppose there's no harm done. I like Jane, you know I do — but I don't always trust her judgement and just want to warn you a little.

Have you been in touch with Jan since you got back? How is she managing on her own? Have you decided to stay apart for longer, or are you planning to move back together, or what? Do let me know. I haven't heard again from Frances — don't expect to, at least for quite a while. I gave her quite a lot to digest and she may not be up to it immediately, if at all. But I think it was worth trying and appreciated your agreeing about that.

Do write. Meanwhile my love and maternal warnings,

Amy

ॐ

Meg to Jane

3 November

Dear Jane,

Thanks for your letter which I waited for eagerly, practically knocking down the postman in my rush to the mail every morning. I've had a thought — why don't we spend Christmas together? Could you come down? Would you like to? It'll only be me and Simon and therefore rather dismal. Jan will pop over sometime, but not for long as she always visits her parents at Christmas. If you think you would like to come, let me know as I have to make plans. If you're not coming, I think I may go away as the thought of being here alone is too depressing to bear.

I'm sorry you think your muddle of feelings is sentimental and therefore not worth having or mentioning. They seem to me perfectly ordinary (that's not meant to be insulting). It's how anyone feels when they're making a new important friendship, or when they're half in love, or beginning to be in love. But I suppose that sort of language frightens you. I dare say you don't believe in any of these tender 'feminine' feelings, but that's no guard against having them!

Let me know what you think about Christmas anyway,

Love,
Meg

ॐ

Meg to Amy

4 November

Dearest Amy,

Thank you for your letter. You're sweet to be concerned
about my emotional health, but do I detect some not-so-worthy
disapproval as well? I know you and Jane have often been on
opposite sides of the feminist fence, but should that be a
measure of one's capacity for friendship or — dare I say it —
love? Nevertheless, I take your point about a Jan-substitute/
Frances-substitute. I must confess, the thought had crossed my
mind as well, in between wrestling with Simon's friends and
staring mindlessly at the box. I can't find an unequivocating
answer. The idea of finding substitutes for human beings is
distasteful, of course, and no one with any dignity would set
about such a thing deliberately, but if the unconscious likes
to behave that way in response to that particular motivation,
what can one do about it?

All I can say is that looking for substitutes was not in my
mind and that the growth of my affection for Jane feels
completely natural, but I can quite see that it may well not
have happened if things with Frances and Jan had remained as
they were.

Another thought has also occurred to me, in this context.
Might it not be time I integrated the sets of feelings I
previously had split between Jan and Frances? For Frances, on
the one hand, the ecstatic, highly-charged, idealistic and
emotional sort of contact which was perhaps kept up by its
not being sexually expressed, and, on the other hand, the
sexual passion gradually metamorphosed into domestic
companionship, but without the continuing excitement of
the first? I sense that, because she is so fiery and interesting,
both these resources might be called into play with Jane. I
don't know. I'm just intellectualising in response to your
question, and in response to my own unexpected intense
feelings. I think Jane must be in more confusion about it
than even I am, since she doesn't 'believe in' all this sort of
emotionalism. Have you heard from her? I'm hoping we

might spend Christmas together and become rather clearer about what is happening.

As for Jan: no, she doesn't want to move back, and I'm more or less adjusted to her living somewhere else now. Simon goes to her two afternoons a week after school and every second weekend, which seems to be fine from his point of view, gives me more freedom than I'm used to, and Jan enjoys very much. Everything between us is very friendly and much better than before. Now when we see each other we can both look forward to it. We don't argue nearly so much and the sexual pressure is, of course, just not there. Her work is going fine and she's joined a local sports club and begun an evening class in exotic cookery of some kind.

I can see she's much happier to have escaped my 'ideological' expectations and I'm not so frustrated by her lack of interest now she's not around all the time. I can't see really that we will want to live together again — we seem to have been travelling different roads for quite some time, but didn't notice the divergence happening. It's a common enough experience, I think, but when people are married they may well accept it with more resignation, since the whole business of divorce is so time-consuming and expensive, not to mention socially disagreeable.

It's so much freer not being married, so much more honest. The terms of the relationship are decided quite privately, without any interference from the State, and the terms of separation are equally private. (Of course, if the State were aware how many lesbians were being supported out of State funds simply because lesbians are all treated as single people, they might make us all get married as they do heterosexuals, but mercifully no one seems to bother about it. They probably think, wrongly, that the number of lesbians in the population is too inconsiderable to bother about. If only they knew!)

Incidentally, why aren't all the heterosexual feminists like you campaigning against marriage? I mean, campaigning against the legal status conferred by the actual certificate? If women were *unable* to marry, and just lived with whom they chose, as you and I do, without any legal consequences accruing from it, then feminists would have achieved half of what they want. Think of it: all women would be equal citizens with men; they would be separate statistics in all the areas the state is concerned with — pensions, tax, benefits and so on. Men would automatically be stripped of the legal privilege conferred by patriarchy, they'd lose their unconscious expectations of being looked after while they earn lots of money — oh, it would revolutionise social life immediately.

Don't you think it would be a better campaign to mount than those long-winded feminist manifestos that no one except feminists are able or willing to read? Wouldn't it quickly polarise the whole community, just as abortion has done, into those who supported and those who didn't? It would be so easy to locate the enemy. No one would be able to sit on the fence — they would have to be for or against. Part of the success of the great campaigns of the past has been due to their focusing on a single issue — the franchise, abortion or whatever.

This whole thing with Jan has made me think of all that's involved in partnership — and how insidious the institution-alisation of sexuality really is. Get rid of marriage — of the *possibility* of marriage — and you get rid of dozens of oppressive evils at the same time. What do you think?

> Much love to you,
> Meg

ॐ

Meg to Jane

4 November

Dear Jane,
I've just written to Amy suggesting we mount a campaign against legal marriage. What do you think? We could all unite on that, couldn't we? It wouldn't matter whether the women were homosexual or heterosexual, we would be campaigning together for the abolition of the marriage certificate, which would strike at the heart of the whole system. I'm so excited

about the idea. How does one book Trafalgar Square for a demonstration? We should have four thousand people burning their marriage certificates, just as the Americans burnt their draft cards. What do you think?

Love,
Meg

ॐ

Jane to Meg

7 November

Darling Meg,

What a great idea! I don't know how you book Trafalgar Square, but count me in. I've even got one to burn, in spite of my divorce. I could burn my divorce papers too.

I don't know any more about being in love and not being in love — what any of it means or not. I just know I think about you all the time and can't wait to see you again. Yes to Christmas, yes to Trafalgar Square, yes to anything you like. Only feel half as besotted with me as I do with you and I shall be more than happy.

Special love,
Jane

ॐ

Amy to Meg

7 November

Dear Meg,

Smashing idea! Yes, it's obvious enough. I've mentioned it to lots of people — mostly women, but some men as well — and everyone said great. Mind you, anyone would — in a jokey way, at least. But you'd better realise what you're up against, and I don't just mean the opposition. Plenty of people are way beyond entering campaigns that are remotely to do with reform and legislation. And plenty of others would argue that women would be left even more defenceless without marriage law — wouldn't many women be even more prey to rampaging men?

Besides that, what's in it for the men? Apart from not paying maintenance, I can't see what they'd gain and they'd have all their domestric comforts to lose. Can you win by just taking something away? Don't you have to put something in its place?

Lots of women see having one man as protection against all the rest. (These are just thoughts. It's not that I'm against the idea — but God, how to do it!)

Still, you are amazing. You sit there with your house and son and traumatic relationships and manage to think up a big new campaign. Think of it — if it did work — if we really could get 3000 or 4000 women — if we really could frighten the Church. . . . I think you're right about it being like abortion in the sense of polarising everybody. The difficulty is not to polarise the feminists.

I'll get people here to put down their ideas and then come and see you about it. The thought of co-ordinating a campaign makes me weak at the knees.

What's happening with Jane?

Love,
Amy

੪

Meg to Amy

12 November

Dear Amy,

I feel overwhelmed. I didn't expect to be deluged with all this enthusiasm. All sorts of people I've never heard of have been phoning up and saying they're friends of yours or Jane's or of other friends of friends. . . saying they want to join the abolition campaign and what can they do? I don't know how to handle it all. Do you think we should have some sort of committee to take it on? I've just taken their phone numbers and told them someone will get in touch with them. What shall I do?

In the middle of all this I am still really only concentrating with one half of my head. The other half is completely given over, whether I will it or not, to thinking about Jane. Well, thinking, dreaming, speculating, fantasising — I can't get her out of my thoughts. I never felt this strongly either about Frances or about Jan. I think it must be the same for Jane. Anyway, we'll be meeting at Christmas. Why don't you and Tim come down then as well? We could get on with the campaign plans at the same time. It's certainly going to need a lot of organising. Just think — Britain could be the first country in the world to abolish marriage, even though it wasn't the first to give women the vote. Everyone then said the suffragettes were crazy, but they don't seem crazy to us now, do they? It could all be the same. What seems crazy now will seem enlightened in a hundred years from now. I suppose we might exempt the Royal Family — let them marry as part of their Tradition. . . .

We will have to think about money — thousands and thousands — for pamphlets and proper advertising and so on. It shouldn't be a little tin-pot flurry that everyone can laugh off. So often women's things turn into that simply because there isn't enough money to do it properly. I think we should try and enlist the gay men — they've got bags of money and never support women's things — well, not very often. But this would be to their advantage as well. It would ensure the equality of civil rights for all citizens.

I think we should make it clear that we're not against people making private contracts with each other — either making vows and promises, and/or drawing up shared tenancies and other legal agreements — all the things lesbians do already. And if people want to have religious ceremonies, and parties, and all that sort of caper, we're not against that either. But none of it would have any status in law. Think, Amy, all children would belong automatically to their mothers. Do say if you'll come at Christmas. Meanwhile lots of love and euphoria,

Meg

Jane to Meg

13 November

Darling Meg,

I'm about to write the first love letter I've ever written in my life. I'm dreadfully ashamed about it and would die if the others found me at it. But I want to and shall. Better late than never.

I think you're right — I must have fallen in love with you. I think you must be right about everything, you wonderful, amazing woman. I never dreamt this sort of volcano-feeling would happen to me. It's so hard to describe. It doesn't seem to focus on anything I'm used to — I mean it isn't specifically sexual, it isn't some intellectual excitement — it's a combination of everything.

I see you all the time — in every sort of mood, every sort of posture. I think only about being near you, with you, and am desperate to be important to you. My will-power seems to have turned to water (not that it was ever very strong!). I don't seem to get angry any more — well, not so much, and not nearly so often. And my principles seem to be sliding into a different pattern that the hard-headed part of me doesn't approve of at all. For example, I catch myself dreaming about living with you and thinking that Simon isn't so bad, as boys go, and we might even have some fun together. I catch myself imagining playing trains with him, or flying kites — honestly, the most sexist fantasies you can imagine!

I hope you can believe in the positive quality of all this 'love' because, quite frankly, it frightens me to death. I feel I'm losing my grip. I'm losing everything I've striven for and built up. And I'm terrified of the others finding out and feeling betrayed, especially when it's always been me who's rubbished such things the loudest.

Help me, Meg,

Yours insanely,
Jane

Amy to Frances

13 November

Dear Frances,

Sorry not to have heard from you but I didn't really expect to yet. In time you will perhaps see that there's some sense in what I wrote and that if I've hurt you, it wasn't with malice.

I don't know if you've been in touch with Meg or not. This is just a short note in case you haven't, to tell you Meg has had the most stunning idea. She has suggested, and has immediately been given a deluge of support, that we instigate a formal campaign to abolish the marriage certificate. If that ever came about — and it would only be after a very long, drawn-out and exhausting effort, we're under no delusions about that — it would make quite a difference, I think, to your perception of your relationship with Jim.

If you had no legal protection of your relationship — if you were in the same position as I am — you might not go to quite the lengths you have in order to blind yourself to some of the more bizarre aspects of your submission to an outmoded idea of womanhood. You might also be more able to identify with women like Meg, and to see that if *all* women were *technically* (as well as actually) at risk from predatory men, it might be easier to establish the sort of solidarity we need. Think about it anyway. Who knows, you might, in the future, even feel willing to lend us your support. History, after all, is not kept at bay because of the private fantasies we might have.

I hope very much that you're all right and working well, and would still like to hear from you some day.

Best wishes,
Amy

Meg to Jane

16 November

My dear Jane,

I've just come running to my desk hugging your 'love-letter', as you describe it, to my lonely bosom, like some smitten adolescent. Lately, amid all the phone calls and so on about the abolition plans, I've been feeling doubtful and had agonies of introspection about whether I'm inventing all this, whether I'm going mad, whether I can manage without seeing you for more than another month. . . . . and so on, and so on. But if you're going mad as well then I feel all right about it!

As for losing your principles — don't worry about it. You'll only lose the ones that don't make sense anyway. Loving someone is enormously creative and positive and validates the essence of one's integrity, if it's healthy.

I'm slightly put out, I must admit, by your cowering in corners and being ashamed to acknowledge me to your friends in the house. I didn't think they were such beasts. I think you should have a go at trusting people and not always thinking the worst. If you've made a fool of yourself in the past by shouting down other women's loves, so much the worse for you. You'll have to admit to them sooner or later that you might have been too harsh, or even wrong, so you may as well get it over with now. The longer you put it off, the harder you'll fall! Take the chance when you tell them you're coming to me for Christmas. Just say we've fallen in love, and leave it at that. If they call you names or laugh at you or get angry, just smile and let them. It's what everybody wants, whatever they say. If they're lucky it will happen to them too. And don't tell me I'm naive — I'm not.

Hugs and kisses and all other sorts of childish nonsense to you — and take care of yourself —

Meg

છ

Jane to Meg   19 November

Sweet Meg,

What a comedy it all is. . . . We sit and argue and read and
tear our hair and when it comes to some mundane event like
beginning a relationship, we all sit and stare. I can't tell you
how confusing everything is. Our house is jammed with
political literature — ephemera, produced by women with
neither enough time or money, on bad paper, full of typing
mistakes, destined for an audience of a few hundred — and
yet there is such passion in all those dry, intricate arguments,
such refinement in the analysis of strategies and of the
process of oppression. I can't turn my back on all that just
because I've 'fallen in love'.

I don't deny that I have — that I must have — but at the
same moment I can read in a dozen different places that
'falling in love' is a mere con — a culture-myth propounded by
capitalism and patriarchy, designed to keep us in our place by
offering that best of all gifts — security. How attractive and
tempting just to fit in, to be part of the larger group, to be
given status and dignity and a sense of worth. I won't just
'lose the principles that don't make sense', as you so naively
put it. Revolutionary cells have, sensibly, insisted on purging
themselves of bourgeois romanticism to strengthen themselves
for the struggle — have embraced what you would call
alienated sex. I *know* why. To be solid, committed, ascetic —
even celibate — gives amazing focus and force to one's efforts.
We can't build a revolution on individual indulgence. We can't
talk about love as if it were a social value. If love is creative
and positive, as you say, then we must find ways to politicise
it. Otherwise people like me will leave the battleground,
retire into private lives and therefore trivialise what our
sisters are trying to achieve.

I know not everyone is made for a life of celibacy — I'm not
one of them and you are obviously another for whom sex is
helpful, even necessary, as a means of contact beyond
language and group activities. But if 'falling in love' means I

should abandon everything I've believed since I became a
feminist then the price is too high.

There must be a way to integrate these two worlds and I
have to find it. There is something dull, I agree, about the
idea of companionship and sharing without the blaze of
passion, but the passion must not be permitted energy and
resources which belong to wider social effort. I mean I can't
and I won't pack my bags and hotfoot it down to your little

We don't *have* to live together, do we? And anyway, how
could we when you have a male child and I have decided not
to give my energies to males of whatever age? Let's take it
easy, try to explore what we're each feeling and wanting, and
not start behaving like a couple of adolescents who know
nothing about the world except the surprise of finding each
other.

You will guess I've been getting a going-over by my sisters
here. But I see their point, as I've just explained. Don't be
angry with me — with us. If there's something important
between us it won't go away and it will bear being analysed
and explored. I want to be with you — don't doubt that — but
I want also to affirm my conviction that feminists are finding
new ways of seeing things, new ways of doing things, despite
the mountains of paper they write and despite the sloganising
they are guilty of. I do love you, but I love them too.

> Your friend and
> sister,
> Jane

ॐ

Meg to Jane

23 November

Dearest Jane,

Thanks for your letter. No, I'm not angry. Confused
perhaps. I don't know why you think a relationship with me
is a threat to your allegiance to feminism. Oh, I understand
the obvious — having less time, putting higher priority on
personal life — that sort of thing. That is the same threat for
any really adult person. One has much more time and energy

for work or for interests or for friendships when there is no
sexual relationship. Alienated sex is fine, but it's not a
relationship and is therefore no threat to anything. It is really
just another interest or leisure activity which takes less time
than going to a movie. A relationship is different — there is a
threat to identity and autonomy because relationship *means*
investing identity, giving up some autonomy — and the fine
balance of how much or how little to give up is very hard to
find. Most people never try, it seems. I agree that it suits
society to pair people off and make them feel safe. How
efficient: the children get born and reared free, the men are
tied down by obligation to keep working at their horrible jobs,
the women trade their minds and their cunts for a relative
degree of safety. But Jane, all that is breaking up — it's been
breaking up for a long time.

In Simon's school, for example, only about half the children
come from that sort of home and only about half the parents
do alienated paid work. *The revolution is already happening*,
don't you see that? No 'moral majority' can halt the
disintegration of the nuclear family.

As the real statistics of rape and child-abuse emerge, as the
black market economy grows, more and more women will
become more and more independent as a matter of course.
You don't have to persuade them with analysis and argument
— only a tiny number of people have ever been persuaded that
way. They are persuaded by events — by the environment
they are living in. All the pamphlets you're talking about do
not constitute propaganda — they are an auditing of the
process *we are already in*, a written record of the experiences
huge numbers of people are *already having*.

The traditionalists are not frightened of feminist polemic,
and why should they be? The pamphlets are unintelligible to
the mainstream bourgeoisie and (dare I say it) equally unintelligible to the proletarian mass whose literacy extends in the
main to the tabloids and the posturing of commercial radio.
Intellectuals, who *are able* to read the pamphlets, choose not
to do so, not wanting to know that the refinement of their

academic ideas does not extend to the grossness of their personal living.

The pamphlets are *religious*, Jane: they are written in an 'in' language, they breathe an 'in' fellowship, they project an ardent commitment — all the things characteristic of a religious consciousness. I don't object to that — it's my religion too. But don't expect the mass of people to be similarly enlightened or converted. Their religious aspirations are tapped by many other religions — and why a person chooses one religion rather than another is about as inscrutable as why they choose one sexual partner rather than another. Every believer knows she has the 'truth' — that is one of the hallmarks.

But be a bit objective about it all. Women are certainly oppressed — you and I know that — although many of them would deny it. Whatever they say or think, however, is relatively unimportant — they are reacting against that oppression with a steadfast and singleminded determination in ways which may be unconscious for them but which the pamphlets are documenting. Every divorce, every laugh at male privilege, every sign of support given by one woman to another — all these things are steps in the process. Every woman who forces her way into the labour market, who says no to bearing more children or to keeping house, is shaking her fist at the patriarchy. Thousands of fists are being shaken — and the thousands will become millions. I want to say that, really fervently, to you and the women in your house. Don't let your ardour blind you to what is really happening.

I know you'll tell me I'm naive again — that rape is on the increase, that women are being pushed back under. It's not true. I live more in the ordinary world than you do and it is all around me. No amount of traditionalism can fight history. Liberation movements progress necessarily. The long haul from the abolition of slavery to the full citizenship rightly demanded by twentieth-century black people is a continuous process. Whatever power, of whatever magnitude, tries to obstruct that process is doomed to fail.

That is not to say I agree with sitting back like God and just watching it all happen. Each act of oppression must be named and fought. But don't lose sight of the whole forest in the struggle with individual trees! If you and I love one another and form our bond that is just as much a tree in the forest as the writing of feminist analysis.

Whatever non-feminist women say, the truth is that every time they do anything independently from men they are asserting their own power and reducing male power. That is why it is ridiculous to fight male *children* — they are dependent on us, not the other way around. If my son grows up to join the enemy, I will fight him, but as yet he is on our side. We nurture him. My female power is paramount.

I wish you would apply a historical perspective a bit more — not just to finding out how the oppression of women has been devised and carried out, and why, but also to mapping the changes we are in. Between my mother's generation and my own, the revolution has already progressed several steps. They could rarely say no to men. Apart from anything else, they had no economic alternative. But huge numbers of their daughters are saying no over and over. My mother lived in her husband's house — I live in my own. So do nearly all of my female friends, whether they are heterosexual or not.

Coming to live with me would certainly be a personal indulgence — if it means simply that you'd prefer it to living how you are now — but that doesn't *preclude* it having a feminist meaning as well. Women need to say no to men — but they need at the same time to say yes to women, don't they? Don't fall prey to some puritan guilt about doing something that gives you pleasure or fulfilment. You need to relax as well as fight.

I've got one of those empty days which means I can rabbit on and on but I'll try and stop now. It's taking so much control to write all these things and not simply say, 'Come to me and let's find out'. Bed is not the only mystery — you, yourself, are a mystery I want to know and never can, not completely. I want to say come to me and be my love. . . .

and then you'll write back and say that's not political! If only
you could see how very political it really is. Oh well.

We can look forward to Christmas at least. Amy and Tim
will be here and we can have a right-on political time
together......

> My special love to
> you,
> Meg

ક•

Frances to Amy

24 November

Dear Amy,

I'm writing to you to acknowledge your letters. You've done
me no harm and although I'm mostly a coward about life I
don't want to become a bitch with it.

But I also want to ask you not to write to me any more.
There's no point. You are so associated in my mind with Meg
and everything that happened that I just feel hurt and angry
when there's a letter from you — I can't help it. My brush
with feminism was enough to put me off for life. Far from
coming around to your point of view I shall probably fight it,
where I can. This world, where I am, is at least sane.

I'll never complain about Jim again — not consciously,
anyway. We have a good life together and he's fond of me. I
can't believe, in my wildest nightmares, that he behaved as
Meg claimed. I think she's mad. She must have been mad all
the time. And I must have been a bit mad as well. But I'm not
mad any more. I've grown up and have grey hairs to prove it.

All that sick, adolescent, romantic lesbian nonsense has
nothing to do with my life or work. I believed her love for me
when it wasn't love at all — just some insane world-view she
wanted to slot me into and nearly succeeded in doing so. I
want to be safe and normal and I'm not ashamed to say so. I
don't want to be dragged into some frightening chaos of
emotion which I can't handle and don't understand. Meg will
no doubt say I have betrayed her for some monstrous man,

but she has betrayed me far more completely by being other than she seemed. I trusted her. I won't ever make that mistake again — not with a woman, anyway.

As for your plan to mount protests against the marriage certificate — I hardly know what to say except that it's mad, like all the other ideas. Marriage is integral to our social fabric and protects people from the hordes of raving mad people like Meg screwing them up about their identities and God knows what when they're much better off getting on with their work and friends and interests. It's mad, too, because it can't succeed. Only a few people will join you and you'll get nowhere and look absurd. Nothing is worth that sort of undignified notoriety.

I don't harm anyone, nor do the millions like me. I sew and knit and write and cook and entertain friends and look after Jim and cuddle my cat and a host of other innocuous or important things. I have nothing to do with mad people — whether it's the Mafia or the CIA or black activists or the IRA or Marxists or feminists. They are all destructive people, disaffected, maladjusted individuals formed into violent aggressive groups and they all want power. If the IRA or the Marxists or the feminists — any of them — were successful and gained the power they want, they would turn round and oppress the very people who they say had previously oppressed them. And I'm expected to take that sort of thuggery seriously! No thank you. One ideology is as bad as another. I want humanist societies, where people can leave each other alone to think and behave as they wish, as long as they do no harm. I want my life as much as you want yours — and I don't want to be oppressed by people like Meg. My relationship with her, incidentally, is the most oppressive experience of my life and miles worse than anything ever done to me by men. I hope you will understand what I mean. It's not directed against you personally.

Best wishes,
Frances

ॐ

Amy to Meg

29 November

Dear Meg,

I'm sending you this letter I received from Frances. You've been so hurt by that whole business I thought you had a right to know what little can be known about what she's thinking. I shall tell her I've given it to you so feel free to respond to her if you wish. Her position seems so entrenched I feel utterly depressed by it and wonder how we can ever achieve a sisterhood when some women think and feel as she does. I suppose we *are* mad — a little. It's so long since I've been close to 'ordinary' women that I'm obviously out of touch with how threatening feminism really is.

What's happening with you and Jane? Don't, please, give in about boy children, at least. I can't imagine you being able to give Simon up anyway, but if you could defend your position with some argument and not just helpless maternal emotion, both your dignity and the cause would be better served. She has no right to demand anything, of course, but it's hard to respect everyone's autonomy when one's feelings are so aroused, I know. Tim and I stayed celibate for a whole year while we were working through our separate demands and expectations. I don't regret it, nor does he, but it was hard. We both wanted, if we could, to find a meeting-point rather than impose our views on one another. It takes a long time. We're all conditioned to treat a lover as a receptacle for our expectations and fears and not to honour each other's 'selfhood'. Jane may not agree. Perhaps it's different between women. Good luck, anyway.

Love,
Amy

Amy to Frances

29 November

Dear Frances,

I know you asked me not to write again but I couldn't let your letter pass without comment. Please understand. I need my self-respect as much as you do and part of mine is taking the space to say what I think and feel.

I've sent your letter on to Meg. She has been so hurt and damaged by what has happened that I thought she had the right to know something of what you are thinking. She, also, is a human being with as much right to her piece of the earth as you or I have. I've told her that I'd tell you I'd sent her your letter so if she decides to write to you you'll know the context.

She is most certainly not mad, and your husband is most certainly a liar, but I see that it doesn't suit you to see it that way. Just think for half a minute, honestly, what reason Meg could *possibly* have for risking a friendship so important to her by making up a web of lies? You must know, if not in your 'wildest nightmares' then at least in your unconscious fantasies, that Meg has told the truth. And you can't take it. Everyone, including Meg, can understand that — and even sympathise — but why you have to be so craven and contemptible as to accuse of her of insanity and hatred when she has been victimised by your husband's brutality because of *his* ego and *his* jealousy, is almost too much to believe.

Your plea for a 'harmless' existence is pernicious, Frances — and I say it in all charity, knowing what lengths women are driven to in order to survive. The life you describe as being so harmless is truly parasitic, real bourgeois intellectualism.

I know the ills of the world are too much for one individual to contend with — and I don't blame you for shrinking from the knowledge of them — but really you *owe* something to the invisible sweat and blood that keeps your leisure life fat and comfortable. How *dare* you say that revolutionary groups are mere malcontents, as if no virtue were possible in their position or in their analysis of their own oppression. You're always so complacent. You probably read novels by Soviet dissidents with the same perverted piety as you uphold the harmless freedoms of decent marriage. Wake up, Frances — you can't stay forever masquerading as an adult in a child's world. Your husband might die or leave you. Marriage is as mortal as anything else — and if you've given your soul to the devil of self-delusion you will suffer, in the end, more dreadfully from your confrontation with the truth than Meg ever has. Whatever mistakes she's made, or will make, at least she's honest. The truth may not make anyone free — but it is the only context we have for negotiating with each other. The rest is mere silence.

I am deeply depressed, even as I write, that I can't reach you, get through to you, that I have to stand by and watch you waste your gifts and spit on reality. But you are still my sister. You belong with us. If you go on supporting male supremacy, it is not — finally — your fault.

> In sisterhood,
> Amy

ह♥

Meg to Jane

1 December

Dearest Jane,
I haven't heard from you for dozens of hours! Please write. At the moment I feel I shall just say yes yes yes to whatever you say, I want you so much. I'm feeling nervous that you haven't replied to my long screed. I imagine you sitting in your kitchen with all the women, going through my letter line by line, looking for political errors. And the others working on your resolve, working on you to forget me and get back to your principles. Please don't let it happen. They don't know everything. I know some things too. I'm right about the importance of bonding — I know I am. We can't win against patriarchy unless we provide some consolation, some comfort, some means other than collectivism to break our

isolation. Add me to the women you have already — if you like — I don't mind — it's not me against them anyway. There's room for them and the political work and me and Simon as well. Don't castrate me Jane. Save the enmity for where it belongs.

I'm also sending you this letter from Frances. She hasn't deigned to address one word to me but this is what she wrote to Amy. I can hardly believe it. I think I could easily kill her. I want to write to her but am too angry just now. What could I say, anyway? What do you think? Oh, do please write.

My love,
Meg

ॐ

Jane to Meg

3 December

My dear Meg,

You silly cow, of course I'm not 'giving you up'. But you were right — we did sit in the kitchen and go through the argument in your long letter. The other women are not monsters, you know — they are not your enemies. And they care about me and my well-being, as I care about them. We're not just flat-sharers, you see — we've been deeply involved in each other's lives and needs and you don't break that sort of bond lightly. I'm coming down at Christmas and can talk at length about what they think and what I think and see what sort of integration we can come up with.

I'm horrified by Frances' letter, although I can remember, about a million years ago, having those sorts of reactions myself. I had a friend, a neighbour, who got involved with a women's group and seemed to me to become more and more mad and fanatical and to foment trouble wherever she went. Her husband left, in the end, and she moved — took her children to some commune somewhere. The whole street breathed a sigh of relief. I remember wondering why she had to be so intense about it all. Frances' letter brought it all back

to me. I'm not surprised by it — but I am horrified. I don't
know what you can write to her — or even if you should. It
may just break open the wound all over again and you'll suffer
and be depressed. And what for? She's not going to see your
point of view — she wants only to preserve her way of life and
her cosy little nest. I feel inclined to say to you just leave it
alone — you've been hurt enough. But you must decide.

I want you and love you,

Jane

❧

Jane to Frances

3 December

Dear Frances,

I've never met you but I know and love Meg and Amy is a
sister. Meg has sent me your letter to Amy which I find
horrifying and feel compelled to respond to, whether you like
it or not. I shall kill your husband if I ever have the chance
and that is no mere threat. Take this letter to the police who
protect your way of life, if you wish, so that you can keep up
your illusion of safety for a bit longer.

You see, I know you better than Meg or Amy ever could, I
mean I know your type, because I was just like you myself
and neither of them ever was. So I know, infinitely better
than they do, that you will not treat what they say seriously,
that you will run away and hide if you can, that you will wipe
Meg out of your life as one brushes away a fly from one's face
when it gets too annoying. So I don't intend to argue with
you. It would be a waste of words. I want to threaten you —
openly and honestly. I want to tell you to watch out. If I can
do anything to destroy the illusion you live in and which
oppresses the sisterhood, I shall. I know who your famous
husband is and that he sometimes has to come to London.
And I am not afraid — not of prison nor of psychiatrists nor of
any of the instruments of your 'decent', 'sane' system.

Neither Meg nor Amy knows I've written this. But I don't
mind if you tell them. I don't mind who you tell or what you
do. Women like you have to be faced with the truth — and if

you won't have it with words, then you must have it with
action. But have it you will.

> In sisterhood,
> Jane

ॐ

Frances to Meg

8 December

Dear Meg,
   I received the enclosed letter from some awful friend of
yours called Jane. She hasn't put her surname or a return
address on it so I'd be grateful if you would send it back to
her. I have nothing but contempt for this sort of childish
melodrama. I suppose it is just a different manifestation of the
madness you all seem to suffer from. As for going to the
police, I wouldn't dream of giving her, or any of you, the
satisfaction of thinking I take any of you seriously.
   Please leave me alone,

> Frances

ॐ

Meg to Jane

13 December

Dear Jane,
   I appreciate your solidarity, but you really can't behave as if
you're some vengeful Electra setting the world to rights by
threat and force. Oh Jane, how could you be so silly? Your hot
temper will get you into some ridiculous wasteful trouble one
of these days. I despair of you. Frances and her bastard
husband aren't worth any sacrifices. I shan't even write to her.
I'm past feeling anything about it all except boredom. So here's
your foolish letter back.
   Come soon.

> Love,
> Meg

ॐ

Jane to Meg

16 December

Dearest Meg,

Just two more days — think of it — and then we'll be together. I'm in such a mixture of moods — anticipation, joy, anxiety, apprehension, this and that — and none of them lasts for longer than about thirty seconds. It's so hard to concentrate on practical things like covering my rota while I'm away and that sort of thing. Lover-woman, you're a witch!

I'm looking forward to seeing Amy, too, and meeting Tim, who had better be as anti-sexist as she says. I don't feel like tangling with some man over my Christmas turkey. The women here have made an enormous pudding for me to bring and send their good wishes.

Irony of ironies — I saw in the press that one of the alternative theatres is doing a play by your favourite male playwright on Boxing Day, and that he will be there. I wonder if he's bringing Frances with him? I'd bet a hundred pounds he isn't. Thanks for sending back my letter — I suppose it was rather silly — but I was so angry and felt it was the only way to get through to her. It didn't work, obviously.

See you very, very soon. Joy!

Jane

&

Amy to Meg

16 December

Dear Meg,

Just a note to say don't do heaps of shopping — we got a car full of fresh veg from one of the women's houses here. They thought they'd be in over Christmas and now most of them have decided to go to a conference in Amsterdam. Looking forward to everything.

Love,
Amy

&

Jane to Meg

30 December

Darling,

It is appalling to be just one day away from you. What an extraordinary time. What a perfect lover you are. I can't imagine now ever being so complete with anyone else. I feel all those banalities lovers are supposed to feel. Thank you for everything. Thank you for existing. For loving me.

You won't like what I'm going to tell you next, so brace yourself. I have sought out the enemy and brought him low. No, don't worry, I haven't killed him or done anything illegal!

Do you remember my telling you that the bastard was having a play on in London on Boxing Day? And do you remember my saying I wanted to stay overnight with an old friend in Hammersmith? Well, I didn't go straight to Hammersmith. I went to the play. I clapped the vain, smiling playwright at the end. He waved and bowed and had a wonderful time with his applause. I went backstage to shake his hand and tell him how wonderful he was. He lapped it all up. I told him I'd met his wife at one of Professor Ball's seminars. He was immediately friendly and asked me if I'd like to tag along to his first-night party, which turned out to be a booze-and-bums private disco in some upper room in Soho. He's the most over-weening man/beast I've ever met — not to be taken seriously at all — a sort of grotesque child. Anyway, you know all that.

My friend in Hammersmith was all prepared, including an infra-red camera, one of those that takes pictures in the dark. (She borrowed it from a friend who's a freelance photographer who goes around trying to find out about missiles and nuclear power stations and all that male crap.)

Between his boasting and posturing our friend felt me up. I clinched it by offering not only my self and my couch but by offering to pay the taxi fare. He said — and you won't believe this! — that that was a healthy bit of feminism he was all in favour of!!! So we went back, and I thought all the time of his ostrich-girl-wife and of my Meg who had been so badly hurt

and I performed better than most pros could, I think, even to
the extent of making sure he didn't penetrate me. And all the
time Betty was busy with the camera through the half-open
door.I hadn't told him anyone else was there so why should
he imagine anything? She made no noise. We had a tape
recorder under the couch as well, so I got the lot. I didn't tell
you for fear of sidetracking our discussions about the anti-
marriage campaign (and other more private delights!) as well
as wanting to be sure the pictures all came out. Well, I've just
got them, which is why I'm writing. You can have a set if you
want but I thought you might find them nauseating. Be
assured that they're good. I've had the tape copied and have
sent a nice parcel off to Frances — am sending today, I mean
— it's wrapped up but I haven't been to the Post Office yet.
I've included a couple of snaps of you and me and Amy which
we took over Christmas so she'll believe I am who I say I am,
and I've told her that you knew nothing of my plan. I dare say
she won't believe that, but so what? There's her precious
husband — caught with his pants down — picture *and* word
beyond doubt.

Now she can have another think about who tells lies and
why and who is mad or not and most of all who knows what
the world is like and who doesn't. He hasn't done anything
illegal — he's just done something he *denies* doing. That's
what I wrote to her, anyway. I'd be surprised if *none* of us got
a response from her, but in case we don't, I'm telling you. I
want you to know.

Just before he left, he asked if he could have my phone
number so we could have another go when he was next in
London. Oh no, I told him. I said I was a lesbian and only
screwed men when there was some chance of getting
something out of them. He laughed. He asked what I would
get out of him. Did I mean money? He said he mostly didn't
have to pay women — he got what he wanted from hot lays
like me. I laughed as well and just said he'd maybe find out
one day. We left it at that.

Now don't be too cross with me. I know you'll say I'm much too dramatic and unhinged and all that sort of thing, but I planned it all in a very cool way, with the women in my house. I explained everything to Betty who also agreed it was the only way. A troll like him certainly isn't worth trying to kill — one may as well be punished for treading on a toad.

I miss you so much already. When can we be together again?

All my love,
Jane .

ဆ

Meg to Jane

4 January

My darling Jane,

How could you!? I want to laugh and cry and bang your head all at once. But my main feeling is one of gratitude for your solidarity, however mad you are or have been — and some sort of mad revenge towards Frances who will now suffer in earnest I suppose. So I want to say thank you and how dreadful of you at the same time. Simon asks where you are. I clutch my pillow in my sleep, thinking it's you. Do come, somehow.

Love, all of it,
Meg

ဆ

Frances to Amy

9 January

Dear Amy,

I don't know if Jane has sent you her obscene photographs or not but I have to write to someone or I'll go out of my mind. I'm too bitter and ashamed to write to Meg — and Jane is obviously some mad Medusa destroying everything and everyone who crosses her path. I suppose she'll destroy Meg as well, not that I care any more. How I wish I'd never met any of you, never heard of any of your ideas, never sat with you as if you were human beings.

I can't leave Jim — I don't want to live on my own. He's fond of me anyway, in spite of everything. I showed him the photographs — he says he was set up. He says he was drugged somehow — something must have been put into his drink — and that he can't remember anything after leaving his first-night party. He says we could take all this filth to the police and say he was being threatened with blackmail but he says he doesn't want the publicity and why make a fuss about such a stupid puerile bad joke. He says Meg's diseased imagination and insane jealousy must have put Jane up to it — that all lesbians are man-hunters who just want bigger and hotter fucks than normal women.

I know he's not a saint — how could he be at his age — but why Meg would want to hurt *me* in this horrible way is beyond my comprehension. The only vestige of feeling I have left for her is to ask you to get her to a doctor and try to get her straightened out before she does any more damage. As for Jane — if she makes a habit of this sort of thing she might find she's biting off more than she can chew. You're not a lesbian — do something about them.

Frances

ẟ

Amy to Frances

14 January

Dear Frances,

I met Jane yesterday and showed her your letter. She told me all the circumstances which you left out and showed me the photographs and played the tape for me. I've told her she shouldn't do such a thing again simply because we don't want to lose her work and energy — she's much more valuable remaining in society than she would be in some prison. She explained that she was infuriated by your betrayal of Meg and that you had to be given the truth in a way you would be forced to take notice of. After she had read your letter I pointed out that people cannot be made to see the truth if they choose not to see it, whatever one does — your letter is proof of that. You can go on believing Jim's lies for ever, if you really want to, however bizarre they are. No one can help you with that — or hinder you. It's your choice and your problem and Jane was wrong to try and force you like that. It doesn't do any good. If you need to go on believing in Jim and hating Meg and living in some private hell you call heaven because you don't dare to try any alternatives, that's your affair. I'm not sorry for you. I can understand, I think.

But be quite sure, if there's any suggestion at all of going to the police or the press, there are many of us who will stand by Jane, and Meg, whatever it costs. I think Jim knows that or he would have hot-footed it to the police already. You will, of course, believe what you must, and if the time ever comes when it is the truth in front of your eyes, then God help you, because no one else will be there to help you. Meg is not alone in despising your dishonesty.

Best wishes,
Amy

ह•

Jane to Frances

15 January

Dear Frances,

By your silence I know you have rightly perceived my motives in revealing your husband's proclivities and have wrongly turned to him for reassurance rather than to your sisters, of whom I am one, whether you accept it or not. The armies we fight are mostly not on some blood-stained battle-field or even in our grubby streets, but in our minds.

One of your husband's motives — a seed planted in infancy to bear fruit in adulthood — is to separate, subjugate and suborn the female sex. Being human he is, of course, capable of affection and companionship — that is perhaps what has confused you. But deeper than that, much deeper, is his desire to hunt, to manipulate and to spread his seed. These are all attributes of power. There is no point in having power unless there is something or someone over which you can exercise it. If you do not feel your powerlessness it is because you do not dare to.

I know what that's like. I was a 'normal married woman' myself. I protected my nest as you have, defended my husband because I thought he needed me to, kept my mind blank of everything except my work, my interests and his needs. (What I thought were his needs.) I made him comfortable when he was tired after his day's work. I cradled him on the odd occasions when he couldn't get an erection. I listened to his theories and suggestions and complaints and analyses with sympathy. I admired him. I thought life was tough for him. I didn't think so much about myself. I didn't feel powerless. I didn't feel anything 'political'.

Then by chance I heard a feminist writer being interviewed on the radio. I was in the kitchen. I was always in the kitchen in the late afternoon, although I wasn't a mother and needn't have been there. I would have felt guilty if he'd come home from work and I was sitting with my feet up, reading a book. He *worked* — I didn't work. I just looked after the housework and maybe wrote. That's what I believed then.

Anyway, I was only half listening but I caught one remark this feminist made. She said 'The man is yet to be born who is not threatened by anti-patriarchal women' — it went on from there — I didn't follow all the argument. But I got the point — that if men really respected their women as equal partners, if they didn't need to feel more powerful than the women, then they wouldn't react with such mockery and resistance against feminism. In other words, if you're not afraid of something you can at least take it seriously before rejecting it.

She suggested that every woman listening should try out some feminist ideas on their husbands and note the reactions.

When my husband came home I did just that, not really
having planned to — just through some psychological reflex. I
tried to talk to him about sharing housework, being
independent, the double standard, I forget what else, and he
reacted first by laughing, then by being bored and, finally, as
if I were taunting him. I was shocked rigid. There was my
nice, middle-class liberal husband talking like some ignorant
fascist and not even being aware of it. We ended up having a
flaming row and spending the first of many nights apart.

He apologised later but I never quite forgot, in all the
months of arguing and fighting and reconciliation that
followed, that initial reaction of threat. He didn't want his
power base undermined, especially in his own home. I tried to
get him to see that it was my home too, but when it came
down to it he said he earned the money so he should have the
greater say. The whole thing was amazingly painful but in the
end I saw the truth. He didn't want me as a real equal — he
had his male friends and colleagues for that. He wanted me as
a wife. He wanted the comfort of my bed, the security of my
homemaking, the companionship of our social life. He didn't
want any of that challenged or threatened. Those things were
his right, somehow. Those were the things he worked for,
paid for. He was somehow entitled to them. That was what
marriage was *for*, he used to thunder at me. Other times he'd
shout, rhetorically, asking what did women bloody *want*? I
didn't know, but I knew it wasn't what he called marriage.

After my experiences with the other women in my house,
who have been better friends to me than my husband ever
could have been, I know what we all want. We want to be
ourselves. We want to find out in our own ways who we are.
We don't want to be told by male doctors and professors and
politicians what we are like and what we want. We don't
want to wear penises, we don't want secretly to be raped, we
don't all want to have babies, we don't find fulfillment in
serving a man's career, and we don't want to be what men call
feminine. What men tell us we want is all wrong. We *do* want
to look after our own bodies, have our own money, make our

own decisions and live our own lives, just as they do. We
want and demand to be independent. If we are ever allowed to
be free, equal and independent — which is *not yet* — we will
find out how we can live in friendship with men.

Why don't you try what I tried. Just *try* it! Say no to sex for
one month and see what happens. Or talk about his making a
donation towards twenty-four hour nurseries — *anything*. Try
it — for the sake of your once-fruitful love for Meg.

I'm sorry Jim is such a shit. But he is — and deep down
you must know it. Be a bit braver — you'll have to be in the
end anyway.

> In sisterhood,
> Jane

ॐ

Jane to Meg

15 January

Darling Meg,

I'm sorry not to have written but I knew you were thinking
of spending a few days with Amy and I must confess I've
pushed down my thoughts and memories of you so I could
start clearing my head and my desk and my life here. I have
a compulsion to get everything in order before letting my
heart run away with everything else.

I don't, basically, *think* it's a good idea for us to live
together — much as I *feel* I want to, like crazy. On the other
hand, the distance between London and the north is so
expensive to cover by train or car that it's impractical to think
of spending weekends together. And you can't come and share
our house — which I'd like better than anything — because of
Simon. So if I don't come and live with you, our relationship
is going to be difficult, if not impossible, to maintain.

I suggest a couple of compromises: first, that you might be
willing to move to a bigger house so that we could set up with
more women, albeit including Simon, and, secondly, plan for
me to come and stay with you for a month, say, to sort out
whether we can live reasonably together or not. That sort of

thing. I don't, very definitely, want to get involved in a lesbian copy of the nuclear family. And I don't want to kiss goodbye either to all I've had here.

Another thing. We've skirted round the issue of monogamy but not really had it out. It looks so bald and cold, I know, just to write these words down. But quite honestly it's easier than when we're face to face. Then everything tends to melt from my mind and I just want to sink into you. I know you'll get impatient and go on about ideology but it's important, Meg. If we really want to make a go of a love-relationship we should be careful and prepare the ground properly. That's something I've learnt the hard way, setting up our house, and I want you to think it's important too.

What we did here, to start with, was agree to keep all sexual relationships outside the house — I mean, not to form sexual relationships with each other. Since we were all committed to lesbian practice, the question of men coming in and out wasn't relevant.

We worked that model for about a year but had to modify it in the end. First, when women went outside to find partners, their commitment to the house weakened — there were always times when they wanted to change the job rotation, didn't want to join in a lazy weekend chat — that sort of thing. On the other hand, when the outside partners joined us — for meals or whatever — the dynamic changed. They half belonged and were half intruders.

So we sat down and re-thought how to manage things. We decided that casual sex really had to be restricted to 'leisure' time and that that had to be stringently kept, so that the dynamic and routine of the house didn't suffer disruption. But for more serious partnerships, the outside partner should be encouraged to join us. If she didn't choose to, then she should only join in at specified social times. It was quite comical in the end: we had to formulate so many rules about all this — to protect every woman's autonomy as much as possible — that we felt rather like a group of women setting up a nunnery, except that our 'Rule' was not to keep sex out but to integrate it safely.

All this assumed that monogamy was not an issue. Two of our women were in a celibacy workshop, anyway, and three of us were divorced and naturally opposed to re-entering any monogamous relationship — that seems to be a fairly standard response of divorced women, whether they're feminist or not. The other three, being life-long lesbians, had already had a series of partners and had lived in female couples before. So sexual relationships weren't passionate and all-consuming (like this one between us threatens to be) and only presented the problems I've mentioned — how they could be slotted into the larger canvas of our work together.

We had all agreed that a sexual relationship ought not to be the basis on which women make commitments and work together. That was one of the functions of feminism — to free women to operate in the world as autonomous individuals. Sexual relationships, therefore, should be private and not carry a social role-playing function, as they do in the heterosexual patriarchy.

All well and good. But what about us? Now I'm in a dilemma. I want to live with you — but only because we have begun a passionate sexual relationship. This is against all the work I've just outlined. *And* I don't want to put my energy into rearing another patriarch. On the other hand, I don't want to deny my feeling for you. That is creative and positive — you're right about that. Agreeing to be non-monogamous would relieve me a lot — although it would be academic, since I don't *want* to sleep with anyone except you at the moment. I just want to feel free — as free as possible. So if we *didn't* live together, and one of us took another partner sometimes, the other needn't be confronted with it. What do you think?

We should feel free to express ourselves sexually as much as in every other way. I'm somehow obsessed with this problem at the moment and have been talking about it to the women non-stop. But it's you I should be talking to.

As for Simon — I don't know what to say or think, and that's the truth. At least I don't hate him or feel badly about him. I must admit I resent his *existence* — the fact of it I mean — as everything would be so much easier and clearer without him. But that's academic too. I'm sure about not wanting to put my *own* energy into his rearing, since I disagree with you fundamentally about the possibility or likelihood of rearing non-patriarchal men. But I respect your right, as a woman, to find your own truth and if you want to devote your energy to that cause, I don't think I have any right to try and obstruct you. I can say what I think and that's all. In practice, therefore, we would *need* to be in a larger group, since with only the two of us it would not be possible for me to detach myself from him. In a larger group I could be friendly and polite but would not have to be *involved*. It seems to me that a larger group is going to be the only way. Expensive train journeys are not on.

I'm depressed by all this. Why can't things be simple? Why can't we get on with the battles against rape and battering? Why can't I just come to you and lie in your arms and whisper sweet nothings and feel that the world is in order? We're all too old, Meg. We're all too scarred and wise and mad. It's cruel somehow that we even try any more.

Nevertheless I love you. In spite of everything I love you.

Jane

ॐ

Meg to Amy

16 January

Dear Amy,

How good I feel after staying with you and Tim — it was certainly the best way to prolong our Christmas together for as long as possible. Simon has enjoyed the break too. Over the last two days he's been asking things like 'Is Tim a mummy?' and 'When I'm a big man will I be like Tim?' He loved sitting in the bath with him too. Is that perhaps something the anti-sexist men could do — show our boy children that there are other ways?

God, the plans for the demo are so complicated, aren't they? I've got such a sheaf of paper after all our talks and the letters that have come in and I'm depressed by the ideological bog we seem to have created. I can't work it all out. As you predicted, one faction says it's 'mere reformism' and would be a waste of energy since even if we did achieve abolition, nothing would be different anyway. Another says it would remove the little bit of protection women *do* have, and that without marriage and rape laws, all women would be prey to unrestrained men and there would be even more abuse. Yet another group says we should leave the law as it is, since, like supporting prostitution, it means we can get the men's money out of them. If we had equal, or greater, economic resources of our own, according to this argument, then we could afford to get rid of marriage — and prostitution — and tell men to go and fuck themselves — literally. There are lots of other twists and turns in what all these letters and reactions present, but the plain message is, as usual, that it isn't clear and straight-forward, which was my original aim.

I really *don't* feel like sitting in endless meetings and forming endless collectives to thrash out all these ideological minutiae. I'm turning into an anti-ideologue, Amy, and if that means I can't be a feminist, then so be it. Or is it really more simple? Perhaps it's just the strain of anarchy that runs through all counter-culture movements? A basic disdain of bureaucracy, a basic mistrust of written rules and procedures, a refusal to use the machinery of the system one is trying to overthrow? Can such an approach succeed? Are these groups of women really going to achieve a circumnavigation of the State itself, and not only survive, but proclaim a new world?

I somehow can't believe it will all happen that way. Yet I can't, in conscience, put my hand to the plough of unreason. Am I too old, too conditioned by my bourgeois education, too earnest for success? Or is this tendency rightly resisted by people like me, representing a lack of experience, a lack of historical perspective, a lack of pragmatism?

For example, I've just got a long letter this morning from one of the lesbian groups saying they won't support an anti-marriage campaign for two reasons: first, because it would mean putting too much energy into something directly concerning men, and secondly, because they are angry that

women can want *any* sort of heterosexual dealings while they
— the lesbian sisters — remain so persecuted. I can't take it
seriously, Amy, despite my natural sympathies with all
lesbians. True, we are persecuted by the patriarchy. But the
cry of rage from these sisters is basically so *conservative*.
They are screaming about *not* having the status their
heterosexual sisters have — and by screaming, they're saying
they want it too. Some of them even want the same legal
recognition of their partnerships which marriage gives
heterosexuals, thus wanting to perpetuate and extend the very
power-relations that marriage endorses! Lesbian women will
get equality when there is *no* marriage — not when there is
more marriage. I despair — but whether I despair of myself, or
whether I despair of these positions, I'm not sure. Is there
nowhere I can belong?

Some of this is urgent at the moment because of my
relationship with Jane. I'm so confused. I've written her so
many letters and not sent them. I'm crazy about her, and yet
infuriated at the same time. Everything is so much simpler in
her world — in her house, they just take no notice of men at
all. Can just forget about male children. I can't not feel hurt
when she is able to push Simon aside, as she does. She hasn't
been *nasty* to him — just neutral, somehow. It's so hard for
me to bear that and I don't even know if I should. Anyway,
what sort of effect will that have on him? Tim was *active*
towards him, and Jane wasn't, and that hurts me and makes
me so angry. Yet I love her and want to be with her and have
to confess life is grey and dull without her, despite all the
things I divert myself with at present. What can I do that's
reasonable? She's entitled to her view, but it doesn't fit with
mine.

And then there has been all that business with Frances —
and Jim. Why did I have to fall for Jane? Is she really just a
destroyer? Oh God, I don't know any more. Sorry to moan. I
loved being with you. Thanks.

Love,
Meg

Meg to Jane

17 January

My dear Jane,

Long letters from you! My heart jumped over when I saw the handwriting on the envelopes and felt the thick wads inside. But I turn cold at all the arguing — the tortuousness of it. People who fall in love, in case you haven't heard, *like* to whisper sweet nothings — I'm not myself too old or wise for that and wish you would regress a little if you need to think such things are childish.

I don't care at all at the moment about monogamy. It is, as you say, academic. There are much more pressing things for me. If you want to sleep with other people, do it. But don't make me know about it — I don't want to. That's your private affair. I can tell you honestly that I don't want anyone but you in my bed and if I can't have you I'm able and willing to sleep alone. I don't think monogamy is anything to do with laying a theoretical base or whatever you called it — it is simply a matter of how one feels. I want you. If I get to a stage when I don't want you, I shall tell you. If I want someone else, I shall tell them. I don't like casual sex — I find it boring. The way male gays carry on about their cruising and 'recreational sex' I find infantile. But if they want to play sex as we play music, that's their business.

I'm much more concerned about how all this is going to affect Simon. I'm his *mother*, Jane. I can't think about him as an object, in the cold way you do. He is my flesh, an integral part of my life. And I'm responsible for him. If I live with you, with the attitudes you describe in your letter, and he *does* grow up to be a 'patriarch', then it will be partly your coldness which *causes* such behaviour. Don't you see? It isn't *possible* to be uninvolved. Everything you do has an effect on other people. Even the Christians have to ask forgiveness for their 'sins of omission'. If you deliberately treat all the Simons with neglect and rejection, you will store up *reasons* for their later revenge.

I'm not talking about protecting or nurturing adult men.

Being adult, they should not be dependent, least of all on women, and they get no succour from me, as you know. Nor do I ask it from them. If that means we are sexually unattractive to one another, then so be it. Neither of us dies because of that. But dependent male children are a different kettle of fish. They are under our provenance — *we* have power over *them* — and we should use it rightly, and enlist as many sympathetic men to support us as we can. Simon has already had a very positive dose of Tim's way of handling things, and I intend to repeat the experience as often as possible. Boys will go on being born, Jane, so you and your women had better think what part you can play in that rather than pretend it isn't happening, or, worse, adding to the misogynistic weight of the culture. After all, our humanity is neglected and rejected by men, and to us that's an expression of the hatred men feel towards women. A boy, who also has an ego — we share that characteristic of humanity — will interpret being rejected and neglected by women as a sign of how much they hate him.

Take the parallel with racism: I understand and accept that I share the collective guilt for our white supremacist past, but when a black person actively hates me because of it, there's not much I can do, and anyway, his or her hatred doesn't exactly endear me to him or her. I can just get myself out of the way and feel sympathetic — I can't do anything else.

Jane, we can't go on merely perpetuating all these evils. We have to *build other ways.* I don't ask you to become a *parent* to Simon — why should you? — but I ask you not to pretend that you can be neutral and not to pretend that being 'uninvolved' will not have an effect on him.

Apart from all I've said, there is the romantic assumption behind your attitude that if I had a *girl* child you would happily put your energy into her and she would *therefore* grow up to carry on our work. Don't be deceived — she could as easily grow up to be a Maggie Thatcher. Our struggle is not yet so established that we can afford to throw away *anybody.* We need everybody with anti-patriarchal potential. I would rather put *my* energy, frankly, into the potential for change represented in my son, than into trying to convert a Thatcher whose male identification is already fixed and inviolate. And defusing all the Thatchers means dismantling their system. Guerilla tactics at the psychological level are fine, but they need to be counterpointed with weapons that the enemy uses and is vulnerable to — and that means a solid phalanx of women and men who will burn marriage certificates and demand larger houses to live in together, as well as carrying on the revolution in bed that is already taking place. Which all amounts to much the same thing: if you want to take me on board, you must take Simon too — at least until he is independent. If you refuse him, you refuse me too. That's how it is.

I've got a heavy heart writing all this — and I want a light one. I want the joy of love and sex and friendship with you. I don't want to do battle with you. I don't want you for an enemy.

I love you, over and over.

                                                        Meg

Amy to Meg

                                                20 January

Dear Meg,

Thanks for your letter. Yes, it was a good time and yes, Tim takes the point about doing more for male children like Simon. We ought to be careful, though, not to work out a too-rigid model — it would become artificial and the children would sense that. We think you should come and stay another week with us soon, if you want to, and talk about it more thoroughly.

I think mostly I agree with you about naive anarchism but I don't think it's helpful for you to become too 'anti-ideological' as you call it. It's necessary to think and write and talk about the 'minutiae'. And don't forget that one of the principles of feminism is the validation of individual women's experiences and thoughts. That means being able to include all the divergent views which women present, as well as avoiding becoming too dogmatic.

There *is* something obnoxious in the notion of sleeping with the 'enemy' — the problem is to agree about who and what the enemy is. For me, Tim is not the enemy, at least not all the time — for others he may be. It's just a much more sophisticated struggle than a conventional male war, where people dress up and invent rules for the game and behave as if their tactics can be made as abstract as algebra. Women have always known that a person's humanity is an inextricable part of the struggle — as men find out too when they engage with an individual 'enemy'. Conventional male armies try to train their troops to become blind to that humanity and to treat the body in front of them as the 'enemy', pure and simple. But thousands of soldiers have reported that when they are face to face with an 'enemy', or have him in prison or whatever, they find themselves unnerved — even undone — by that man's expression of emotion, photographs of his children, and so on.

Male armies and medical professions and the whole paraphernalia of 'professional training' are still trying blindly to stamp out this fundamental humanity. Women know, have always known, that that is not only impossible and undesirable but that it is also evil and counter-productive. The minute you reduce your 'enemy' to the dimensions of a piece of algebra, you're lost — and your cause is also lost. You might manage to kill that particular human being, but a hundred will spring up in his stead, and you can't kill them all.

What is necessary is to *work* with that material and *change* it — infinitely more difficult but in the end the only method which has potential for success. The enemy is patriarchy — and like its evil allies, capitalism and fascism, it will have to be defeated on its own territory, which is people's minds. That means, finally, changing the political machinery, the education system — the whole diseased projection of male culture. More and more women are outraged — and a few men too — by what those institutions perpetrate and condone — the battle in their minds has already begun.

The feminists you are impatient with are providing the weapons we need — new ideas, different resources, an unmitigated rage. If they feel that what you, or I, or any other woman, suggest to be priority strategies, are really — in their view — mere diversionary tactics, then they are right to protest. Expect it, Meg — it's part of the process.

I don't know what else to say about you and Jane. The time we all spent together was positive in the extreme and she is now so much more a rounded personality for me than when I first met her. All I can suggest is that you work through the problems in living, rather than trying to hammer ideas at each other. The reality isn't much like the ideas anyway, as you and I know — especially when it comes to living with children. The more she has to deal with Simon as a young child, the less he will become an embodiment of the patriarchy. She's sensitive enough to know that, and may be resisting for that very reason. If you want to keep your hands clean from the pollution of dealing with the enemy's humanity, it's better never to know him, and certainly better never to have cuddled him after a bad dream or wiped his bottom.

Let her come to terms with it her own way, Meg — you don't get anywhere with argument. It was like that with Tim and me — we argued a lot in the beginning, and only got exhausted and resentful and frustrated — then, very gradually, we learned to work through each situation as it happened. The most helpful thing we learned was to try not to generalise each other's attitude and potential. If Jane wants to engage with you, she will have to engage with Simon as well. If she can see that, it will be sufficient. She will say yes or no to you both. In some better world, where adults shared children properly, such a statement wouldn't be necessary. But as it is, he's your child and she will accept that or not, as she can. Cold comfort, but you know how it is anyway.

Love and solidarity to you,

Amy

Frances to Jane

22 January

Dear Jane,

I've had your letter. I've thought long and hard about whether to answer it or not and finally decided it was best to write to you.

Although we've never met, I'm in the strange position of feeling more anger towards you than I ever have towards anyone. Whether Jim was drugged or not, you manipulated him in order to hurt me and that is very difficult to forgive. In fact, I don't forgive you. The nasty imprint of those horrible pictures is still in my mind. You have presented me with an ambiguous piece of information and, whatever the truth is and whatever it means, I would rather not have known. None of you, including Meg, respected that. You think you have some God-given right to shove people's faces in what they say they don't want to know about. Well, you haven't got that right. And because you haven't, I want you to understand, and to make Amy and Meg understand as well, that whatever communication any of you might send me in the future, I shall not acknowledge. I won't write to any of you again. It will be for me as if you never existed.

I have decided to take a fellowship in Boston for a year, to clear my head of all this and to get on with my work. Jim will stay here. You have not succeeded, as you were determined to, in breaking up our marriage. You have simply introduced some poison into it which will take some time to evaporate. I am grateful for one thing only — and that is your telling me about your marriage. At least I could see from that that some part of you is, or once was, human. I hope — for other people's sakes — that you and your fellow-travellers will reflect a little on what you've done and what your motives really were. Has it occurred to you that you might be so angry with conventionally married people like me *not* because of your stupid ideology and phony revolution, as you claim, but because your own marriage failed and you are consumed with bitterness? Just because it didn't work for you doesn't mean it can't work for me, and millions of other women. You have no right to try and smash up our lives just because your own has been such a mess.

You say you were provoked by your 'love' for Meg — if that's a measure of lesbian 'love', you'd be better off finding a new husband and trying to get straight whatever went wrong before. You're like all lesbians — you build your lives on rejecting men and declare war on any woman who refuses to do the same. If there *is* any point to lesbian love — and I used to think there was, before all this nightmare began — then surely it must have to do with supporting women and caring about them — not trying to destroy them.

I have the comfort of knowing I'm more civilised than you are. That I can give you the satisfaction of knowing I shall think about these things while I am away from Jim. I can tell you as well that I have grieved deeply for my lost friendship with Meg. But I did that privately — with dignity, I think. If you could only do things in ways which were not destructive to other women's lives, then I might believe in your so-called 'sisterhood'. At present, I don't believe in it at all.

> Goodbye,
> Frances

ॐ

Jane to Meg
                                        30 January

Dearest Meg,

I'm sorry to have taken such an age to write — well, that's not strictly true, since I've written you a letter at least once a day but haven't posted any. Now I must. Apart from what I want to say, I wanted you to have this letter from Frances as soon as possible — it came this morning. You will see from it that nothing more can be done on that front — the best we can hope for is that her year in Boston helps her somehow to find her independence. That, fairly clearly, is that.

About Simon: I know there is something right in what you say but I need to fight it. That's about as honest as I can be. I don't want to give you up. I've tried, over the last week — not

posting letters, trying not to think about you, burying myself
as much as I could in everything up here. But it's no use.
There is something in our relationship together — its potential
— which I want and am not willing to let go. If it means I
must accommodate myself to Simon then I'll get on with it.
But be warned that I'm angry about being pushed — even if it's
by my own feelings — into that particular corner. I shall be at
war with myself over it. But if I let you go, I shall be at war
over that, equally. That's what I've worked out over this past
week. So if I have to be at war, it may as well be with the
assistance of a love-relationship as without.

I know that is a very narcissistic thing to say. I haven't said
anything about what Simon might feel about it, or how it
might affect him. Frankly, that is more your concern than
mine. I've had no experience in living with children or
bringing them up — remember that. What you say about
female children turning into Thatchers is too painful to
contemplate. You may be right. But you haven't said anything
about getting a bigger house. I think if you insist on your
point about Simon, you must allow me to insist on mine
about needing a larger group and a larger space. That way we
shall have physical and psychological support and not be
forced to depend too much on each other. I can't make any
promises about anything until you agree to that.

I suppose you're right about monogamy. I just feel better
and can handle things better if I know what the ground rules
are from the start. Perhaps it's no more important than a
personality difference. For you, feelings are everything and
any hint of ideology makes you suspicious. All right — so
long as I have my theoretical freedom, I can be happy.
Whether I choose to act it out or not is my own concern, as
you say. I wish, nevertheless, that you'd see *some* value in
discussing these things. Not everyone is brave enough to exist
on a diet of feelings alone — and, anyway, people quite often
find that their feelings carry them into places they don't like.
Don't be over-romantic, Meg. A dash of romanticism — your
style of it — is appealing, but too much becomes oppressive.
Can you understand that?

I miss you like crazy. I want to come and see you next weekend but one. Will that be all right?

All my love,
Jane

≈

Meg to Amy

31 January

Dear Amy,

I've been chewing over your letter and one from Jane that arrived today. It seems you're right about her knowing it's got to be Simon and me or neither of us. She wants — insists, really — that the only way it would work, though, is in a larger house with more people. I've been looking at estate agents' lists and finding out about squats and so on — I haven't yet told her I agree, but I think I do. All this pressure on couples living in isolation is too much to be borne. I'm nervous about saying it: but — what about you and Tim joining? Don't just say no — maybe it's even a way of ameliorating lesbian oppression, apart from other things. If only men like Tim would put their money where their mouth is, so to speak. Give us their extra money or their protection or whatever else they've got. Will you at least discuss it?

I've done a quick survey of the groups who want to support the Trafalgar Square demo — at a rough reckoning there would be at least eleven hundred people. May seems to be the preferred time — preferably just after the May Day march — the second or third. Quite a lot of money has come in — we can pay for stamps and printing but we really need a worker. It's too much for me to handle on my own. Another reason for us to share a house!

Enclosed is Frances' 'goodbye' letter to us all. She sent it to Jane. She's a sort of stranger to me now.

Love to you,
Meg

≈

Meg to Jane

31 January

Dearest Jane,
   Thanks for your letter and for sending the one from
Frances. I've sent it on to Amy. Yes, that's that.
   I agree about the larger house. Sorry not to have said so
sooner — I wanted to check out the finances and also to ask
Amy whether she and Tim would join us. Don't rage about
Tim — it would be good for Simon to share with him and it's
an act of solidarity towards Amy. We have to start somewhere
building some bridges. If they say yes, I want them. Will you
agree?
   I've seen quite a lot of Jan lately — mainly fixing up
finances and talking about Simon. She's quite happy with her
flat. That's another thing that seems to have ended. Is that all
that happens? Just a trail of relationships, one leading to the
next? I feel depressed somehow, despite all my hopes which
are fast becoming centred in you. But you won't let me
become too dependent, I know. I can sense it. The
combination of your thoughts and my feelings might just be
the right formula for success. Yes, I'm a romantic from way
back. I want a base — I don't want to feel like a drifter.
   Do come at the weekend. I want you to come. I need you to
come. I feel I've known you all my life. You are an integral
part of me. My future belongs with yours. Oh, I know we
won't hold hands and drift into the sunset — but we're strong.
We can do it.

I love you,
Meg

Amy to Meg

3 February

Dear Meg,
   Thanks for sending Frances' letter. So, she's cut loose. One
has to wish her luck in the abstract. She's not the only
woman having to re-think. But it's too much for anyone to do

alone. I hope she comes across some support in Boston. We'll never find out, I suppose.

I'm not frightened about sharing a house with you and Jane — nor is Tim. But there are the inevitable boring, necessary practical things to be worked out — jobs, schools — and so on. We've talked about it before but there was never a real chance to it. We're free to come down to London for the first weekend in March. Can we come and stay with you then and discuss it some more? Could Jane come too, do you think?

Eleven hundred for the demo sounds like a good enough start — it could be a lot more than that by May. When/if we meet in March we could plan how to co-ordinate the campaign, whether to get a worker or not, and so on. March will be an active time, dealing with the outer world.

At the moment I feel I need time and space for my inner world. So much has happened. I need to digest it all. Tim and I are taking two weeks off from next Monday and going to the Mediterranean. Winter is winter wherever you are — but I need a change of scene. Look after yourself — see you in March, I hope.

> My love to you,
> Amy

ह**

Jane to Meg

3 February

Darling Meg, .

Silly to write. I'll be seeing you in a couple of days. There are things so hard to say face to face. Hard for me, I mean. My tongue isn't used to saying them, perhaps. It's just that I've woken up today with such an enormous feeling of gratitude and well-being. Everywhere outside is covered in white — it must have snowed half the night — so as I'm in picture-postcard land, I'm having picture-postcard feelings.

I want you Meg. I covet you, as they used to say. It's so right to be with you, so wrong not to be. I want to say yes to

everything — yes to you, yes to Simon, yes to moving to
London, yes to life. I won't be cutting off everything here —
I'll bring it with me. These women and my life with them are
in my bones, in my heart, in my head — they're part of me.
And now you're part of me as well, and I love you. It seems so
simple this morning — as simple and unpredictable and good
as the snow falling. I honour you. You are good and right for
me. With you I shall be more who I am. I love you for that, as
well as for yourself.

   Goodbye only for now — and then hullo,

                                          Jane

                        ළ♥

Meg to Jane

                        5 February

Darling Jane,
   I've had your snow letter and you're about to arrive and will
have this waiting for you after our time together. Now, and
then — before, and after, I say yes to you Jane — yes — yes —
yes. . . . Come soon. . . come quickly. . . stay with me,
and go, and come again, and go, and come again. That's how
it is, that's how it really is. That way there is always enough
time, always enough space. . . . I love you. I feel embraced
by you and I embrace you in turn. Keep safe, my sister and
friend and lover. Your woman's power is like my own — we
need not fail.
   I want to be where you are,

                                          Meg

Sheba Feminist Publishers

Sheba is a feminist publishing cooperative, formed in March 1980. All our books are available by mail order from Sheba, 488 Kingsland Road, London E8. Please add 45p per volume for p&p. Write for our catalogue of books, cards and posters.

Other books are

Sour Cream, Jo Nesbitt, Liz Mackie, Lesley Ruda, Christine Roche. A collection of feminist cartoons, 2nd edition. £1.75.

The Ten-Woman Bicycle, Tricia Vita. Illustrations by Marion Crezée. A charming story about how women enter a 'man's world – together. Particularly suited to children. £1.25.

Woman and Russia, translated and with an introduction by the Birmingham-based Women and Eastern Europe Group. The first feminist samizdat, published in Leningrad in December 1979 and immediately suppressed. This is its first appearance in English, £1.95.

Smile, smile, smile, smile, Alison Fell, Ann Oosthuizen, Stef Pixner, Tina Reid, Michele Roberts. A collection of feminist poetry and short stories illustrated with drawings by the writers. 'As my moods change from elation to self-irony to depression and back again, I find poems here to comfort and affirm my experiences.' *Feminist Review.* £1.75.

Feminist Fables, Suniti Namjoshi. Drawings by Susan Trangmar. An elegant and subversive collection of stories that rework mythology as it *used* to be . . . they create an uniquely feminist pattern of meaning. £2.25.

Spitting the Pips Out, Gillian Allnutt. As if entries in a notebook, painful, humourous, despairing, hopeful, this collection of poems, prose and wry comments tell the story of one woman's journey towards selfhood. Though the story is autobiographical, many women will recognise it as their own. £2.25.

Loneliness and Other Lovers, Ann Oosthuizen. A novel of changes, heartaches and discoveries as Jean ceases to be 'someone's wife' and builds her own life, for herself. £2.75.

The Great Escape of Doreen Potts, Jo Nesbitt. An irreverent children's book written and illustrated by feminist cartoonist Jo Nesbitt, with sturdy heroine Doreen outwitting everyone in their attempts to marry her off to the stupid prince. £2.50.

For Ourselves, Anja Meulenbelt. A radical new look at women's sexuality (translated from the Dutch). Richly illustrated with photographs and cartoons, the book is a joyful celebration of who we really are, what we really look like, dismissing once and for all the passive Playboy image that has for so long been called our sexuality. £4.50.

Sour Cream 2. A new collection by thirteen feminist cartoonists: provocative, hilarious, thought provoking. £1.75.

Our Own Freedom. Maggie Murray. Introduction by Buchi Emecheta. 'These photographs of women in Africa show that the basic things of life – obtaining water, fire, shelter, the care of the young and the sick – are almost entirely done by women. These are the basic necessities of life and yet there is little or no compensation to the women who do them. Because they are unpaid, such tiring and boring chores are called 'women's work'. These words come from Buchi Emecheta's introduction to Maggie Murray's photographs of women in Africa. £3.75.

Girls are Powerful, edited by Susan Hemmings. A collection of radical writings by young women from *Spare Rib* and *Shocking Pink* magazines. The pieces in this collection are written by young women from seven to twenty-two, but they contain ideas which will open up discussions between women of all ages – perhaps for the first time. They burst through the notions of what young women can and can't think – to change us all. £3.75.

Rocking The Cradle: Lesbian Mothers, Gillian E. Hanscombe and Jackie Forster. This book looks at the many different ways in which lesbian mothers conceive and bring up their children against the background of a hostile society, and suggests that the way of life of these women has significance for everyone's future. The women interviewed here are but a small group of pioneers – but what they have done, and what many others are continuing to do and say presents a powerful challenge to the nuclear family as the basis of western society. £3.50.

Everyday Matters – New Short Stories by Women. The stories we have chosen for this book have one thing in common: they do not sit comfortably. Each in its own way questions or resists the story we were all brought up on – the one that told us how we feel and what we want and who we are. The stories are varied, provocative, sometimes violent, occasionally humourous. Many are by women who have never published stories before. We hope this book is a beginning for a new wave of women writers. £3.50

Funny Trouble by Fanny Tribble. A new book of feminist cartoons from the woman whose first collection *Heavy Periods*, was a huge success in 1979. Three years later her humour is just as biting as she gives us a cool and ironic look at men and babies and feminists. Fanny is not afraid to confront the conflicts between heterosexuality and feminism, and this, coupled with her ability for self mockery, makes this book an appealing and challenging read. £1.50.

The Playbook for Kids About Sex. Words by Joani Blank, Illustrations by Marcia Quackenbush. A bold and startling book about sex for the over 5s. Illustrated throughout with line drawings and using the school work book format this innovative book encourages and expects the readers to personally involve themselves in an unusually lively and friendly discussion about sex. £2.